Can Democracy
Safeguard the Future?

T0070435

Graham Smith

Can Democracy Safeguard the Future?

polity

First published in 2021 by Polity Press

Polity Press
65 Bridge Street
Cambridge CB2 1UR, UK

Polity Press
101 Station Landing
Suite 300
Medford, MA 02155, USA

ISBN-13: 978-1-5095-3924-6
ISBN-13: 978-1-5095-3925-3 (pb)

A catalogue record for this book is available from the British Library.

Typeset in 11 on 15pt Sabon
by Fakenham Prepress Solutions, Fakenham, Norfolk NR21 8NN
Printed and bound in Great Britain by CPI Group (UK) Ltd, Croydon

The publisher has used its best endeavours to ensure that the URLs for external websites referred to in this book are correct and active at the time of going to press. However, the publisher has no responsibility for the websites and can make no guarantee that a site will remain live or that the content is or will remain appropriate.

Every effort has been made to trace all copyright holders, but if any have been overlooked the publisher will be pleased to include any necessary credits in any subsequent reprint or edition.

For further information on Polity, visit our website:
politybooks.com

Contents

Acknowledgements

This book has been a long time coming. Short-term demands have got in the way of its completion. The irony is not lost on me.

The ideas in this book emerged not only from academic conversations, but from political engagement. I am privileged to be the chair of the Foundation for Democracy and Sustainable Development and have had the pleasure of working with and learning from fellow trustees over a number of years. It does feel as if the policy window is slightly ajar. Whether we are able to force it open is another question. I would like to thank past and present trustees and associates for the inspiring conversations that have helped to develop my ideas. I can also thank future trustees, whoever you are, because the organisation will be necessary in

Acknowledgements

the years to come. Additionally, I have been fortunate enough to work closely with numerous impressive democratic practitioners and activists who, through their actions, have shaped my thinking about the potential for participation and deliberation. I am humbled also by fellow rebels in Extinction Rebellion, who inspire me with their courage and creativity in the face of the climate emergency.

I have presented ideas in this book at numerous academic conferences and workshops. Thanks to everyone who has offered critical reflections. I would like to single out Michael Mackenzie for particular appreciation. Some years back, I had the good fortune to be a visiting scholar at the Ash Center at Harvard University at the same time as Michael. He had recently finished his PhD on future publics – a much revised version of which is soon to be published. Our long and inspiring conversations made me realise that I might have something to say on this topic.

Finally, the greatest source of encouragement has been my family. Susan pushed me to work on the manuscript when other short-term commitments seemed more pressing. She is inspirational and my most supportive and loving critic. I dedicate this book to three wonderful representatives of

Acknowledgements

the world to come: my niece Marianna and my nephews Alex and Matthew. It is their future and the future of those who follow them that is my most significant motivation.

1

Failing to Deal with the Long Term

Democracies have a blind spot when it comes to the long term. From issues such as pensions, health and social care, and infrastructure through to climate change, biodiversity, pandemics, and emerging technologies, we find repeated failures to develop robust policies that safeguard the interests of future generations.

Climate change has become the paradigmatic case of short-termism. Over decades, democratic governments have been warned about the long-term impact of climate change and the need to reduce drastically emissions of greenhouse gases and to invest in adaptation. Their response has been painfully slow. In the 2015 Paris Agreement, the world's governments committed to reducing warming to 2 degrees centigrade above preindustrial levels, with the aim of achieving only 1.5 degrees of warming. The more radical 1.5 degrees ceiling requires net zero emissions across all nations by 2050. According to the Intergovernmental Panel on Climate Change (IPCC), realising this ambitious goal will entail 'rapid and far-reaching transitions in energy, land, urban and infrastructure (including transport and buildings) and industrial systems'.[1] The UK government has led the world in legislating for the net zero target. Yet the Committee on Climate Change, empowered to report regularly on the government's progress, has questioned its commitment and its capacity to achieve this goal.[2] No democratic government has seriously embraced the necessary long-term structural change that achieving net zero requires.

While 1.5 degrees warming will significantly reduce the likelihood of catastrophic impacts of climate change, extreme weather incidents such as flooding and heatwaves, species extinctions and sea-level rise will still increase, threatening livelihoods over decades, particularly for the poor and most vulnerable. The record of democratic governments on capital investments in implementing infrastructure and natural disaster defences is poor, which suggests that the building blocks for more concerted climate adaptation are not in place. Many democracies are plagued by utility distribution systems and transport networks that are near breaking point. Capital spending too often papers over the cracks. The pressure on governments to respond to more frequent natural disasters is rising, whether these be the impact of drought and bush fires on communities in Australia, hurricanes in the United States, more regular and intense flooding in the United Kingdom, or heatwaves in unprepared cities around the world. Democratic governments can often put in place impressive disaster response operations, but the planning and investment that would protect vulnerable communities from the social and economic miseries that natural disasters bring in their wake is too often lacking.

Short-termism is also generating major social policy dilemmas. The ageing populations of our democracies place particular strain on health and pension services designed for previous eras. A focus on acute hospital-based treatment means that preventative services are often underfunded. Children's services that ameliorate problems early, public health strategies that promote healthy living, and social care services that enable long-term conditions to be managed in communities are starved of money. In the United Kingdom, governments have continually avoided dealing with the social care crisis. Official report after official report has been published, but politicians are unwilling to act. At the same time, political parties compete over how much they will invest in the health service – never enough to keep up with the increasing demand caused by the lack of preventative action in other policy domains. Austerity cuts reinforce these false economies, placing further strain on acute care in hospitals. As the Health Foundation argues, '[a] failure to take a long-term view of the value of investments that promote and maintain people's health means that recent trends in government spending are storing up problems for the future'.[3]

The recent COVID-19 epidemic is a final example that highlights how a lack of long-term thinking can have negative systemic impact. The failure of many democracies to plan effectively for pandemics increased the death toll and put health and social care services under intense stress. Democracies have been forewarned. Building on previous intelligence assessments, the US Director of National Intelligence stated a year before the outbreak that 'the United States and the world will remain vulnerable to the next flu pandemic or large-scale outbreak of a contagious disease that could lead to massive rates of death and disability, severely affect the world economy, strain international resources, and increase calls on the United States for support'.[4] Similarly, the Global Preparedness Monitoring

Board – an independent monitoring and advisory body convened by the World Bank Group and the World Health Organization – warned in 2019 that trends such as global air travel and climate change significantly increase the risk of a pandemic. The report lays out plainly the imperative to build strong, coordinated, and well-financed response systems.[5]

A clear theme emerges. Inadequate policy responses to climate change, infrastructure, health, and pandemics are just four examples of 'democratic myopia' – the tendency towards short-term thinking in democratic decision-making. We could reflect equally on the failure to consider burdens placed on the future in areas of policy as disparate as pensions, housing, education, and nuclear waste and in emerging technologies such as nanotechnology and artificial intelligence.[6]

These various policy challenges share similar characteristics: they entail immediate costs designed to ensure long-term gains. In more traditional areas such as health and pensions, some gains will be felt immediately by those directly affected by the policy change. Other areas, such as education and infrastructure, can take more time to realise benefits. The temporal characteristics of climate change are particularly challenging. Any effective response requires that extensive costs be borne by current generations, so that generations yet unborn may benefit. The time lag between action and its consequences means that current generations will not witness the fruit of their endeavours.

In all policy areas, not acting stores up problems for the long term. From a purely economic perspective, it is generally more efficient to act now than in the future. The Bank of England has estimated that between $4 and $20 trillion assets could be wiped out if the climate emergency is not tackled.[7] The much lauded Stern review *The Economics of Climate Change*, commissioned by the UK government in 2006, provides clear and unambiguous evidence that the benefits of strong, early mitigation considerably outweigh the costs of not acting.[8] The review estimates that unabated climate change will cost 5 per cent of global GDP each year (more dramatic predictions run as high as 20 per cent). In comparison, the cost of reducing emissions would account for only 1 per cent of global GDP. A similar story can be told for natural disasters. Estimates from the United States suggest that every $1 spent on preparedness is equivalent to about $15 of the future damage it mitigates.[9]

Long-term challenges are not simply technical problems to be solved by experts. They generate significant ethical conundrums. Political decisions need to be made about who gains and who loses. Policy options have differential effects within and across generations. A common tendency is to view future generations and their interests in aggregate. For example, different policy responses to the climate emergency will place varying burdens on current, near future, and far future generations. This assumes that different generations have their own collective interests. Such an assumption is deeply problematic. As Simon Caney argues, it 'tolerates outcomes in which some lead appalling lives'.[10] It fails to recognise that, within future generations (just as in our own), significant imbalances of power will exist, with different vulnerabilities to policy impacts across social groups. National income statistics such as GDP aggregate costs and benefits, hiding significant differences in well-being within and across the current generations. The economic pie may get bigger, but the slice available to the poorest may be getting smaller. Increases in GDP can mask accelerating inequalities. The same will be true for future generations, if we consider them in aggregate. Policy choices have distributional effects, creating and reinforcing differentials in social and economic power and vulnerabilities *within* and *between* future generations. The

IPCC provides clear evidence that current decisions on the mitigation of greenhouse gases will affect the number and location of people vulnerable to sea-level rise, heatwaves, and food shortages. Our decisions about adaptation strategies entail political choices about what social groups in what locations and in what generations to favour. Technical expertise takes us only so far. Political judgements have to be made about the relative weight that should be given to the interests of different social groups across space and time.

The drivers of democratic myopia

Contemporary democracies are not fit to make political judgements that deal fairly and effectively with the long term. Why does democratic governance seem unable to deliver consistently over time? What is it about democratic institutions that drives myopic, short-term policymaking? Why are the long-term challenges in the 'too difficult' box?

The explanation is multifaceted. At least four characteristics of democratic systems engender democratic myopia: the absence of future generations; the electoral cycle; entrenched interests; and the broader capitalist system.[11] I will consider the effect of each of these characteristics in turn. While my focus here is primarily on the nation state, these drivers affect decision-making at higher and lower levels of governance.

The first challenge to long-term thinking is that, quite obviously, future generations do not exist. Future generations are not present within democratic institutions to make the case for policies that safeguard their interests. They cannot put political pressure on current decision makers. Feminists have long argued that women's and minority groups' lack of presence in democratic institutions has led consistently to decisions that do not take their interests into account. As Anne Phillips argues, 'when policies are worked out *for* rather than *with* a politically excluded constituency, they are unlikely to engage all relevant concerns';[12] hence the argument for political strategies such as women-only or minority-only shortlists for legislative seats. With presence comes a more meaningful consideration of the interests of previously politically marginalised social groups. With future generations we are in a bind. Whereas the proportion of women and ethnic minority groups in legislative assemblies can be altered, we cannot simply extend the politics of presence to the politically excluded constituency of future generations.

Any democratic design to promote the interests of future generations will have to be a second-best solution. If future generations cannot represent themselves in political decision-making, some form of surrogate representation is necessary. Surrogacy brings its own challenges. Surrogate representatives cannot be authorised and held accountable by the constituency they aim to represent – in this case, a constituency that does not yet exist. Epistemic and moral challenges emerge as claims about the interests of future generations are made in their absence, together with predictions about the consequences of our actions.[13]

A second institutional driver of democratic myopia is the electoral cycle: electoral terms are relatively short – between four and six years (two years for the House of Representative in the United States). The electoral cycle can have a number of effects. Most obviously, politicians and political parties have a constant eye on the next election. Success in electoral politics requires evidence that candidates are able to deliver clear benefits to voters at the next election. Bearing costs in the present for the sake of benefits at some point in the future is not generally perceived as a vote-winning strategy.[14] A compelling study of disaster preparedness in the United States indicates that voters do not reward congressional politicians for investing in policies that prepare communities for natural disasters. Investment had no positive effect on the likelihood of re-election. By contrast, the release of relief funds in response to natural disasters was a significant predictor of increase in an incumbent's vote share, even though the estimate is that preparation is 15 times more cost-effective.[15]

The preference for short-term action for electoral purposes is reinforced by the compliance problem that governments face if they wish to embed long-term strategies. Decisions play out over decades, and in view of this require the consistent application of policy over time. Present administrations cannot bind future governments. No guarantee can be provided that policies will be continued over the long term.[16] Our current partisan politics makes compliance over time even more challenging. Decision makers cannot force the hand of those who follow them.

Electoral calculations by politicians rest on the idea that voters are themselves myopic. Voters are taken to prefer short-term benefits, and governments must be responsive to those preferences. This is a powerful storyline that politicians and political parties tell themselves. The short-sightedness of individuals has been a preoccupation of economists and psychologists.[17] Economists have long propagated a model of the individual who has positive time preferences: people place greater value on enhancing or protecting their welfare now than in the future. The model of *Homo economicus* informs policy tools such as cost–benefit analysis, in which future gains and losses are discounted by comparison to those accruing in the present. According to such tools, policy options that bring immediate benefits and defer costs are those that generate value to society – and these characteristics are the polar opposite of long-term policymaking. Government decision-making is structurally informed by tools that systematically favour immediate economic gratification. Psychologists point to various human traits that work against the long term. Optimism bias, for example, means that individuals underestimate long-term challenges and overestimate their capacity to respond to change; negativity bias tends towards placing more weight on the costs of interventions. Mainstream economic and psychological perspectives imply that myopia is hard-wired. Dennis Thompson articulates in a common observation the challenge that this situation generates:

> Most citizens tend to discount the future, and to the extent that the democratic process responds to their

demands, the laws it produces tend to neglect future generations. The democratic process itself amplifies this natural human tendency.[18]

While such accounts of the public attitude towards the future have a significant impact on the judgements of decision makers, their explanatory power is limited. Consistently, studies of attitudes to the future have shown that time preferences are highly sensitive to context and framing.[19] The standard economic model is not as universal as is so often assumed. The tendency to privilege the immediate is part of our everyday reasoning, but this is not a necessary condition. Psychologists draw an important distinction between two systems that are present in the mind.[20] System 1 is automatic: it constitutes our immediate response, without voluntary control. In contrast, system 2 requires attention and effort; in it we take time to consider and reflect on alternatives. It is impossible to function by putting all decisions through system 2 reasoning – we would never get anything done! Neither is it correct to assume that humans are simply hard-wired to act myopically. Sociologists have long argued that time preferences are affected by the social practices in which we find ourselves embedded. Context matters.

Can Democracy Safeguard the Future?

The earlier example of natural disaster management in the United States suggests that short-term
considerations win out: officials who respond to
natural disasters as they happen are rewarded, officials
who invest to protect the population from the effects
of natural disasters are not. On careful examination,
this state of affairs may be less driven by positive time
preferences and more to do with the salience of the
issue. Investment in long-term policy does not grab
the headlines, whereas acting decisively in response
to a disaster captures public attention. Andrew Healy
and Neil Malhotra found that the only time investment paid politically was when it took place in the
immediate aftermath of a significant natural disaster
such as Hurricane Katrina, or when it was part of
a grassroots disaster preparedness programme that
engaged local stakeholders.[21] Salience counts. The
problem for many long-term challenges is that they
often do not have that salience. The climate crisis is
a perfect example. It does not obviously and materi-
ally affect the daily lives of most citizens in advanced
industrial democracies. As a creeping problem, it fails
to capture attention in the same way as other policy
issues. Movements such as Extinction Rebellion (XR)
have to resort to high-profile civil disobedience to
bring these issues to the forefront of political and
public concern.

Experimental research by Alan Jacobs and Scott Matthews challenges the simplistic view that the population has little interest in the long term. A more powerful driver of voters' unwillingness to support long-term policy is uncertainty.[22] Uncertainty expresses itself in two forms. First, it is shaped by the complexity of the issues at hand. Long-term policy challenges are typically complicated to understand and often require complex policy interventions. The higher the causal complexity of a policy intervention, the more uncertainty it generates among individuals. Will it really work? The higher the degree of uncertainty, the less likely the support is for the policy.

This combines with a second characteristic of uncertainty: a lack of trust in governments that they can see through long-term action. Partly this reflects the problem of electoral cycles that we have already raised. When a policy requires compliance from future governments, how can the public be confident that it will be supported by those who follow? The compliance problem is reinforced by lack of trust in politicians in general. Measures of trust in politicians and mainstream political institutions have been dropping over time, with specific evidence that the public believes that politicians act in their own interest rather than for the collective good. Testing particular explanations of distrust, Will Jennings and colleagues find that the public considers politicians to be obsessed with capturing short-term media headlines and to be overly influenced by established interests, so much so that democratic politics no longer represents the interests of everyday citizens.[23] If the context is one in which the electorate does not trust the actions of the political class, democracies are in crisis when it comes to safeguarding the future. The bias against long-term action among voters is not so much to do with positive time preferences or psychological traits as it is driven by uncertainty and distrust.

Even if economic and psychological models of short-termism are suspect, they continue to structure the judgements of politicians and political parties. In the run-up to elections, parties compete to 'buy off' sections of the population with short-term promises. A prime example is the calculation that UK political parties have made to protect pensions. In recent elections, both governing parties and opposition parties have advocated a 'triple lock' under which pensions will increase by 2.5 per cent per year, or in proportion to the rate of inflation, or in proportion to average earnings – depending on which one is higher. The short-term interests of older voters are prioritised, as the latter are more likely to turn out at elections. By comparison, young people, who vote in lower numbers, are faced with rising student debt and increasing housing prices that reduce their living standards.[24]

A third characteristic of democratic institutions that drives short-termism is their responsiveness to interest groups. The pressure that interest groups are able to exert shapes the political agenda. Powerful incumbent groups that have a strong material interest in retaining the status quo are most difficult to shift. They resist change. As a result, long-term policymaking often requires disruption of their privileged position. The prime example is how those who profit from a carbon-based economy – especially fossil fuel companies – have resisted moves towards a more sustainable, low-carbon economy. It is oil companies and other actors with a material interest in sustaining the carbon-based economy that bankroll influential organisations and individuals to promote climate scepticism and outright denial, sowing seeds of doubt among politicians and the wider public. Reflecting on the challenge of taking forward climate policy, James Ashton, one-time UK government's special representative for climate change, has stated: 'Where there is a contradiction, the forces of incumbency start with a massive advantage.'[25] Many of these interests have strong material and social connections with democratic governments: they fund political parties and individual politicians directly. Extensive analysis of the winners and losers of policymaking in the United States offers robust evidence that it is the wealthy and organised business groups that gain most from government decision-making. The working class and the middle class seem to have their interests fulfilled only when they align with the wealthy.[26] Established interests act as a brake on change. Future generations have no constituency with anything resembling this kind of power and influence.

The government itself is divided into an array of different departments and agencies with competing interests. Long-term policy requires coordination. Set this need for coordination against the ongoing competition for limited budgetary resources. Departments and agencies act in silos, with little concern for the activities of others or for the external costs of their decisions. For example, the failure to invest in early intervention means that England and Wales spend nearly £17 billion on taking children into care, on dealing with the consequences of domestic violence, and on providing welfare benefits to young adults. These costs are borne by a variety of public agencies that are not responsible for causing the long-term problem.[27] Established patterns of power and spending across government are difficult to shift and align for consistent long-term policymaking. The impact of new public management (NPM) philosophies across the public sector has worsened the situation. A multitude of agencies has responsibility for discrete issues; these agencies are disciplined by annual appraisals against specified targets. Such a context actively demotivates more strategic coordinated action.

The popular idea that government is well placed to make reasoned and strategic decisions has long been challenged in political science. Charles Lindblom's classic remark that governments 'muddle through' is apposite. Democratic governments constantly have to balance different and often competing interests, both within and without, in order to act. According to David Runciman, it is the capacity of democracies to muddle through that, historically, has been critical in dealing with immediate political crises. It gives democracy a certain flexibility and adaptability as power dynamics shift. But, when it comes to long-term challenges that require more considered and planned responses, muddling through is of very limited value.[28] In the face of such problems, muddling through is often nothing more than resistance to systematic change.

A final set of explanations of short-termism in democratic politics focuses our attention on the ways in which broader cultural and economic dynamics shape the activities of democratic institutions. Norms and practices associated with contemporary speculative capitalism militate against long-term thought and action. We have already suggested that entrenched economic interests can thwart long-term policymaking through overt or covert political strategies. The argument here is that democratic institutions are more deeply constrained and conditioned by the discursive dynamics of capitalism. Capitalism shapes the way we think about and conceive of the world, such that certain ways of being and doing are taken as given. Our earlier discussion of NPM is illustrative of the existence of a strong discursive commitment on the part of democratic governments – a commitment often referred to, loosely, as 'neoliberalism' – to leaving decisions to the market. Market logic is celebrated over state action in the distribution of scarce resources. However, markets are a place where short-term economic interests prevail – where short-term return on profit will often trump long-term investment. Business leaders are increasingly judged by the criteria of short-term share price and market value. Performance-based pay structures tied to short-term return create perverse incentives.[29] The extreme implications of such a logic were made visible after the recent financial crisis. Banks and other financial institutions that caused the crisis through their short-term investment strategies in search of immediate profits were bailed out. Austerity was enforced instead of investments in the future being made.

Short-term economic performance comes to exemplify progress in the form of national income accounting: this is what nations judge their comparative standing against. As already noted, such accounting often hides extreme income inequality across social groups. The way in which GDP and other measures are calculated fails to value the extensive unpaid caregiving and community action that underpins healthy social relations. Similarly, pollution and biodiversity loss are taken as externalities of profit-seeking behaviours. Our measures of progress valorise short-term economic return and rapid consumption over the conditions for long-term social and environmental well-being.

Short-term logics abound in the contemporary media environment, which continually demands new content. Politicians and political parties feel the need to feed social media and the news cycle constantly with instant opinion and novel policy announcements rather than to promote a stable policy environment across time. The media environment is also complicit in selling a 'good life' that implies rapid and ever-increasing consumption over restraint and concern for the long term. Immediate gratification trumps long-term sustainability.

The absence of future generations, the motivations generated by short electoral cycles, the constraining hand of entrenched interests, the insidious impact of speculative capitalism: all these various constraints placed on democratic institutions limit their capacity to act so as to safeguard the future. How are we to respond to the drivers of democratic myopia? We are faced with a blunt choice: ditch democracy or reinvigorate democracy.

Time to ditch democracy?

Ditching democracy rests on the argument that democracy has had its chance, but has proven itself incapable. A stronger hand is needed to push through the necessary sociopolitical changes for long-term governance. This authoritarian perspective has been particularly vocal in the face of the ecological crisis. The language of 'climate emergency' may reinforce this trend, although XR, which is complicit in this trope, sees it as a driver for deeper democratisation. Writers in the 1970s argued that restricting freedom is necessary if we want to avoid ecological breakdown. Democratic processes are too slow to respond, and our individual rights and freedoms generate 'collective selfishness and irresponsibility'.[30] The climate crisis has reinvigorated authoritarian thinking, highlighting the flaws and contradictions in democratic institutions and laws and the influence of corporations in market societies. For David Shearman and Joseph Smith, the drivers of democratic myopia can be overcome only through a form of expert-led authoritarian governance.[31] Singapore and China are often held up as exemplars from which we can draw inspiration for a centralised control by technocratic elites.

This call for authoritarianism is finding some resonance in the scientific community. Appeals to our 'exceptional circumstances' abound. The influential author of the Gaia hypothesis, James Lovelock, makes the case against democracy:

Even the best democracies agree that when a major war approaches, democracy must be put on hold for the time being. I have a feeling that climate change may be an issue as severe as a war. It may be necessary to put democracy on hold for a while.[32]

Similarly, Lord Martin Rees, Astronomer Royal and former president of the Royal Society, has argued: 'Only an enlightened despot could push through the measures needed to navigate the 21st century safely.'[33] Pleas to bypass democratic institutions can be found across different areas of policy where frustrations exist about failures to act.

The appeal to autocracy has major limitations as a political response to our current predicament. In part it rests on the assumption that the removal of electoral dynamics will ensure stable long-term policy. This neglects the presence of the other drivers of myopia, which are reinforced by the dysfunctionalities specific to autocratic regimes. The long-term policy record of autocracies is not promising. The intergenerational solidarity index, developed by Jamie McQuilkin, captures the capacity of different types of political regime to address long-term economic, environmental, and social issues. Working with Roman Krznaric, McQuilkin has applied the index to comparing democracies and autocracies. Out of the top performing 25 countries, 21 are democracies; out of the lowest 25, 21 are autocracies.[34] Similarly, Frederic Hanusch offers compelling evidence that democratic qualities of states tend to correlate with improved performance on climate policy.[35] Democracies may not be effective in safeguarding the future, but they outperform autocracies. Outliers exist. Communist Cuba's long-term investment in social policy is a favoured example. Advocates such as Shearman and Smith argue that the evidence for the poor performance of authoritarian regimes is not relevant as they typically accommodate themselves to capitalism and the destructive practices and dynamics that this brings in its wake. Theirs is an argument for a different type of autocracy.

What is the likelihood that benevolent and far-sighted authoritarian rule will emerge and be sustained? The record is not promising. The hierarchical structures of authoritarianism generate governance dysfunctionalities, as they lack veto points where decisions can be challenged and new ideas considered.[36] Where long-term policies are enacted by autocracies, they often favour particular social groups over others as regimes attempt to solidify their support. Elites in such dominant positions do not have the incentive to provide long-term public goods and will appease those interests that help sustain their position. At the same time, highly centralised power is always under threat from usurpers with less benevolent motives.

Hierarchical structures are more likely to erode rather than to nurture the kind of reflexivity and experimental disposition that is key to preventing crises and to adapting to changing conditions. The closed settings of autocratic government tend to suffer from 'group think' and are poor at learning and adaption. Corruption and clientelism undermine the flow of good quality information around the political system.[37]

Conclusion

Disenchantment with democracy is on the rise. Surveys from democracies across the world offer evidence of growing illiberal sentiment and support for non-democratic solutions.[38] While the extent of disillusionment is debated, this is a worrying trend, which points to a lack of confidence in democratic institutions. The authoritarian diagnosis rightly points to the failures of democracy in realising effective long-term governance. It is unclear, though, why the kind of structural change proposed as an alternative – centralisation of power in the hands of an autocratic leadership strong enough to push through the required policies – would fare any better.

If not authoritarianism, then what? The answer is not to dispense with democracy per se. Yes, democratic institutions as currently constituted have a tendency towards myopic decision-making. But is this a necessary condition of democratic design? We are the inheritors of democratic institutions that do not look that different from those of the nineteenth century. They were not designed to respond to the range of long-term policy challenges we now face. Democracy does not need to be abandoned. Its institutions need to be reinvigorated and restructured. Designed for the long term. As John Dewey argues, 'the cure for the ailments of democracy is more democracy'.[39]

2

Reimagining Established Institutions

If the problem is that the interests of future generations are inadequately considered by democratic
institutions, can this tendency towards short-
termism be 'designed out'? Can we purposely reshape
democratic institutions so that future generations
are given due weight in decision-making? This
chapter considers modifications to the structure
and practices of two long-established and defining
institutions of democracy: the legislature and the
constitution. In considering the redesign of these
institutions, we are interested in how structures
and practices might encourage decision makers to
consider the future in their political judgements.

Many of the design propositions that I discuss in
this chapter remain thought experiments – proposals
that have not made it off the drawing board. In a few
instances, we can learn from the practice of actually

existing institutions. The aim of this chapter – and of those that follow – is to consider the extent to which the design of democratic institutions can be effective in altering the temporal orientation of political judgements. To what extent can restructuring institutions ameliorate the different drivers of democratic myopia? In designing institutions, we need to be cognisant of the effect that this can have on their democratic legitimacy. The danger is that altering institutional structures and practices might undermine democratic credentials. Similarly, we need to assess the feasibility of proposals more broadly – not least how practical it is to envisage the institutionalisation of reforms.[1]

The legislature

For contemporary representative democracy, the legislature plays a critical role in legitimising the political system as a whole. The legislature is the body that embeds the principle of political equality, at least formally. Any citizen has the right to stand for election to the legislative assembly. Every citizen has the same power in the selection of representatives: one person, one vote. In practice, of course, political equality is far from realised. Only members of major political parties have a realistic chance of electoral success. We end up with a political class that tends to share similar social backgrounds. The structure of the electoral system affects the relative influence of voters on the composition of the legislature. The general rule is that more proportional systems provide for a wider range of political parties to represent different social interests and ensure that votes are closer to equal weight. Alan Jacob's work on the implementation of pensions schemes within advanced industrial democracies suggests, perhaps counterintuitively, that the more veto points there are within a political system, the more likely it is that the system in question will deliver outcomes that are sensitive to long-term considerations.[2] The combination of proportional systems, the coalition governments that typically result, and federal arrangements will tend to promote a more effective long-term governance. This is confirmed by research on environmental outcomes, although the results are not consistent across all areas.[3] The suggestion is that the more consensual a political system is, the more capacity it displays for dealing with long-term policy challenges. This is only relative. Most of the time, most legislatures are driven by short-term concerns and fail to attend systematically to the long term.

Many of the drivers of democratic myopia relate to the actions of elected representatives. Relatively short electoral cycles motivate politicians to focus on policies that have a visible return before the next election, or that promise immediate returns just after. Changes in government every four to five years reduce the credibility of long-term commitments. How can politicians and voters be sure that the promises of one administration will be followed through by those that follow? The inability of future generations to stand for election or to vote means that their interests are not represented within the body. Without a social group's presence, its interests are rarely fully considered and safeguarded. The influence of interest groups on the work of elected officials reinforces the status quo. It is as if legislatures and other elected offices had been explicitly designed to undermine long-term thinking.

In rethinking legislatures, a number of design options emerge that respond to different aspects of democratic myopia. These options can be distinguished by the extent to which existing electoral rules and membership remain unchanged. Proposals either focus on the internal practices of the existing legislature, leaving membership intact, or look to more significant structural change, aiming to reform the electoral rules or the characteristics of representatives.

Parliamentary committees

The Parliamentary Committee for the Future in eduskunta (the Finnish parliament) is perhaps the best known example of reform within the current structures of a legislature.[4] Established in 1993, it has gained the international profile of the first permanent parliamentary committee to have the consideration of the long term across all policy areas as its core mission. The committee is unusual in that it has no explicit legislative responsibilities: it does not scrutinise government bills. Other committees can request its advice, although this happens rarely. Its main obligation is to respond to the Government's Report on the Future, which is published once every electoral term. These reports have been on themes such as Finland's changing external environment, the country's place and role in the world, the impact of an ageing population, realising carbon neutrality, sustainable growth, and the future of work. This scrutiny function places the committee in dialogue with the government. While the Report on the Future and the committee's response to it come rather late in any government's term, they can have an agenda-setting effect on the governments that follow. Outside this required function, the committee is free to determine its own agenda and practices. Most of its time is taken up by its own inquiries. The reports that emerge have relatively little impact on the everyday activity of eduskunta.

The committee's independence from the legislative timetable and tendency to select less politically controversial issues for its inquiries have led to a comparatively non-partisan, deliberative, and consensual style of working. This has contributed to the longevity of the committee. It is no threat to the work of the government, political parties, or other committees. Even though the immediate impact of the committee is limited, its different way of working and its more strategic orientation ensure continued interest among parliamentarians in being members of it. The committee is recognised as an important training ground for politicians in their early career. Significant individuals, including prime ministers, have credited the time they served on the committee with opening their eyes about long-term challenges and shaping their thinking in this area.

Other countries have adopted committees with similar characteristics; the Parliamentary

Advisory Council on Sustainable Development in the Bundestag is one such example. It is not clear why the German parliamentary committee has not achieved a status similar to that of its Finnish counterpart. One possible combination of explanatory factors is the relatively small size of eduskunta, the relatively consensual style of Finnish politics, and the way in which the structure and practices of the Finnish committee promote cross-party deliberation. The explicit focus on the future rather than on sustainable development is also a potential explanatory factor. 'Sustainable development' can be interpreted as a more politically loaded term, in which environmental considerations are given priority.

The Foundation for Democracy and Sustainable Development (FDSD) has made the case for a Committee for Future Generations in the House of Lords in the United Kingdom.[5] This is a very specific legislative context: a rare legislative body with appointed members that does not work under the constraints normally generated by elections. The potential to take a longer term view by comparison with the elected House of Commons is a common justification for the existence of this non-elected chamber. At present the House of Lords has no internal infrastructure to express that function systematically. FDSD argues that a Committee for Future Generations should be given a more prominent legislative function than we see in the Finnish model – namely the right to scrutinise any legislation that the committee deems may have significant impact on future generations. Whether this risks the politicisation that the Finnish committee has avoided is an open question. Party discipline is weaker in the unelected House of Lords, and committees less partisan and more consensual. The Well-Being of Future Generations Bill that has been proposed in the United Kingdom makes the case for a cross-parliamentary 'committee for the future', which would consist of members of both Houses.[6] Institutional design faces the challenge of balancing the desire for a non-partisan culture against the potential to impact the legislative process.

The Scottish Futures Forum, established in 2005, draws inspiration from the Finnish committee, although it takes a very different form. The forum views itself as the independent futures think-tank of the Scottish parliament, bringing together both parliamentarians and external experts from academia, civil society, and business. Its positioning as an independent body beyond the electoral cycle aims to stimulate debates on the long-term challenges and opportunities that face Scotland.[7]

The creation of parliamentary committees with an explicit mission to promote long-term thinking is certainly feasible – after all, the Finnish committee has existed for over a quarter of a century. What we have yet to see is a committee that has legislative bite.

Electoral rules

A number of design proposals suggest structural change to electoral rules and practices. One set of proposals takes as its object of concern the shortness of an electoral cycle, making the case for longer terms of office for parliamentarians. Another set focuses on the electorate, aiming to rebalance the bias in favour of older voters either by disenfranchising them or by enfranchising younger voters. Yet another approach aims to ensure the presence of legislators who are more likely to protect and promote the interests of future generations. In all these cases questions of political feasibility and acceptability emerge.

If one of the drivers of democratic myopia is the shortness of electoral cycles, then lengthen the terms of office: extending the period will remove some of the electoral pressures faced by politicians.

The longer the terms, the easier it will be for far-sighted policies to be established. A longer term does not get over the problem of temporal compliance completely – policies need to be in play over decades; but it gives time for policies to be embedded. Politicians will not feel under the same degree of electoral pressure to show short-term gains, so they may be more considered in their policy-related decisions.

Longer terms generate at least two democratic challenges. One is practical. How feasible is it to expect the electorate to accept fewer opportunities to remove governments, at a time when trust in government and in politicians is at such a low ebb? The other concerns politicians. Would their behaviour change? Their record to date suggests that they tend to privilege the interests of the wealthy and powerful, except at moments when politicians themselves are publicly accountable – that is, during regular elections.[8] Extending electoral terms may have the unintended consequence of putting even less of a brake on the tendency to privilege entrenched interests. While short electoral cycles are a driver of short-termism, it is not clear that simply lengthening those cycles produces positive long-term effects. Any effects of reducing electoral motivations on democratic myopia may be overwhelmed by unintended negative consequences.

I also mentioned a set of electoral proposals that focus not on how often we vote, but on the characteristics of the electorate itself. The electorate of most democracies is ageing. As life expectancy has increased, older voters have come to outnumber younger voters. This demographic shift is reinforced by the lower proportions of younger voters who turn out at elections. Parties recognise these patterns and consequently appeal to the short-term interests of older people. The protection of pensions in the United Kingdom, in comparison to the relative lack of attention to policies designed to improve the well-being of younger generations, has already been mentioned as a prime example. A self-reinforcing logic is at play: younger voters believe that their voices are not being heard, and hence do not participate in elections; but this increases the influence of older voters.

What is to be done? Radical proposals have emerged. First, change the nature of the electorate, so that the bias in favour of older voters is removed.[9] This can be achieved by disenfranchising the elderly or by increasing the voting power of the young. The idea here is that the younger the electorate is, the more interest it will take in longer term policymaking, in enlarging its horizons. While the first option, to disenfranchise the old, is an interesting thought experiment, it is hard to imagine older people wishing away their voting rights. Democratically, it is also a retrograde step: the history of democracy has been accompanied by an expansion, not a reduction of suffrage and political equality.

An alternative thought experiment moves in the opposite direction: enfranchise even younger voters. As David Runciman has provocatively argued, if the problem is an older electorate, reduce the voting age: instead of starting at sixteen, as we see in a number of polities, go as low as eight.[10] A common reaction to this proposal is that young people simply do not have the capacity to understand the issues at stake in elections. How should one respond? One solution is to give parents more votes: people with children should get to vote on their behalf. However, no evidence exists that parents are more long term in their thinking than the rest of the population. The idea that some members of the polity would be given more voting power on the grounds that they have children could well have perverse consequences: if you want to have more political power, have more children! Besides, a movement is emerging of concerned young people who commit to not having children because they are worried about the future, given climate predictions. Such people would have less electoral influence.

Another reaction to the proposal of enfranchising younger voters is to suggest that this move would lead to a less cynical electoral politics. Ask young people what they are concerned about, and the fate of the planet and education will come high up. Runciman suggests, amusingly, that the tenor of public debate would certainly improve if politicians have to go to schools and appeal to children. Voting for the first time while still at school is one answer to the question of how to encourage younger people to get into the habit of voting. If you vote once, you are more likely to vote in the future. If one of the duties that we have to future generations is passing on a thriving democracy, then young people with electoral practices inculcated in them would seem to fit the bill.

These various suggestions for enfranchisement remain thought experiments. The evidence that young people are naturally more long term in their thinking lacks firm empirical support. Nevertheless, enfranchising the young would rebalance inter-generational inequities within current generations, bringing the policy concerns of younger people more squarely onto the political agenda. Still, the impact of enfranchisement on the interests of generations yet unborn is unclear. Such thought experiments are useful for clarifying dysfunction- alities in our existing democratic practices, but whether they can generate the necessary political support for institutional reform is another matter. Extending the franchise any lower than the age of sixteen looks improbable in the present political and cultural context, although the actions of youth climate strike activists are changing the tenor of the debate.

A third and final set of proposals I mentioned revolve around the absence of future generations from legislative bodies. The answer is to create dedicated seats for representatives who promote the interests of future generations. One option is to rebalance the age profiles of legislators by intro- ducing in parliaments a quota of seats for younger representatives. The current age profile of parlia- ments militates against the interests of the young.[11] Again, the assumption that younger people are by definition more long term in their thinking and actions is contested. While such a move could well recast the balance of power across existing generations, it may do little for the longer term beyond bringing different perspectives into any parliamentary debate on what the interest of future generations entails.

A more radical set of design options suggest setting aside seats for surrogate representatives of future generations. How could this be done? Andrew Dobson initiated the debate with an argument for specific representatives of future generations who would be elected to the legislature by a proxy electorate.[12] His suggestion is that active supporters of environmental groups should make up the proxy electorate: their support for such organisations is evidence of a needed long-term orientation. Unsurprisingly, Dobson's idea has courted controversy, not least on account of the inference that all long-term concerns can be reduced to environmental sustainability. The long-term policy agenda is much broader and much more contested. Dobson also hedges on the issue of whether members of the sustainability lobby would have two votes or would have a choice between voting for a traditional representative and voting for a future generations one. Either option would undermine the idea of equality in suffrage and, from a sociological perspective, would further empower white middle-class citizens, who tend to be the supporters of environmental groups.

Kristian Ekeli offers a simpler and more democratically acceptable proposal: all citizens would have two votes, the second one being for future generations representatives.[13] Ekeli sketches out how the dynamics of such a mixed legislative chamber might function. The proportion of future generations representatives does not need to be large (he suggests around 5 per cent), particularly if they are given the power to delay legislation when a qualified majority of these representatives vote against a measure. Ekeli suggests that the threat of delay would engender an anticipatory internationalisation of the interests of future generations among other representatives. Governments would be incentivised to put forward policies and legislation that look more systematically into safeguarding the future, in order to counter minority action. Ekeli admits that the main challenge to his proposal is the suspicion that political parties would game the system and, as a way of increasing their control over the legislature, would put up future generations candidates who may not be concerned about the long term. He contends that legal norms would need to be developed to ensure the formation of future generations parties that are separate from traditional parties. Such norms would be enforced by the courts in the same way in which they already consider the suitability of representatives or guardians of children. The idea of different types of representatives is not entirely far-fetched: the Italian senate includes a small number of senators who are selected by expatriate Italians. In this case, the innovation is to give a vote to Italians who live abroad. The idea of having two votes for different kinds of representatives is a qualitatively different design proposal.

More recently Ekeli has proposed a different strategy, which would not involve the potentially controversial creation of separate representatives of future generations. Instead, sub-majority rules would enable a sizeable minority within the existing legislature – at least one third of its members – to delay, or to require a referendum on, a bill they believe threatens serious harm to posterity.[14] The proposal would yield a mechanism for minorities to put a brake on activities detrimental to future generations. Minorities would function as 'watchdogs for posterity in present political debates and struggles'.[15] Ekeli believes that this would have a similar, anticipatory impact on legislation and policy. To ensure that minorities do not abuse the power to halt government business and deploy it for purely partisan electoral party motivations, he argues that a constitutional court or some such

44

body would need to be empowered to resolve whether a *prima facie* case of potential harm to posterity has been presented. The power to delay legislation and to pass the decision to citizens is a theme to which I will return as the argument of the book develops.

The proposals I have considered so far focus on revising the terms of office, the age profile of the electorate, the type of the representative, and the rules of the legislature. All have accepted the basic principle of elected representatives. An alternative proposal suggests that politicians and political parties should be removed, since they are the root of the problem. In one fell swoop, short-term political party electoral pressures and the need to pander to vested interests would be eradicated. Instead of elections, we should look to the ancient practice of sortition – random selection – as the constitutive principle for legislatures.[16] A randomly selected chamber would take a longer term orientation, because members would not be affected by the pressures faced by elected politicians. The proposal may not be as fanciful as it may first appear. It is one where evidence can be drawn from the existing practice of randomly selected bodies such as citizens' assemblies and juries, and where a small but vocal constituency is making the case for sortition legislatures.[17] I will leave further exploration and critical discussion of this idea to the final chapter and its focus on embedding more systematic citizen participation.

The constitution

The adoption of constitutional protections for future generations has gained traction, not least because of the number of states that have revised or written their constitutions in recent decades. Constitutional provisions can take a number of forms. The most basic are general statements of responsibilities towards future generations that often appear in the preamble. More substantively, where rights for future generations are being entrenched, they are often framed in relation to environmental protection or sustainable development. For example, Norway's constitution affords environmental rights to future generations:

> Every person has a right to an environment that is conducive to health and to natural surroundings whose productivity and diversity are preserved. Natural resources should be made use of on the basis of comprehensive long-term considerations

whereby this right will be safeguarded for future generations as well. (Article 110b)

The Hungarian constitution refers to future generations at a number of points, obliging the state and every person 'to protect, sustain and preserve' natural resources for future generations. Similarly, the South African constitution recognises the right of future generations 'to an environment that is not harmful to their health or well-being'. Particular policy outcomes that are substantive and long term can also be embedded, most commonly in relation to fiscal rules. The most well-known are commitments to low sovereign debt levels in a number of European countries, including Germany and Sweden. While such provisions do not explicitly mention future generations, the effect is to place a limit on the debt we pass to those yet unborn.

Among proposals for constitutional strategies for the safeguarding of posterity, Robyn Eckersley argues for the entrenchment of the precautionary principle.[18] The principle has a number of competing definitions, but the version within the Rio Declaration is widely recognised: 'Where there are threats of serious or irreversible damage, lack of full scientific certainty shall not be used as a reason for postponing cost-effective measures to prevent environmental degradation.'[19] The principle has appeal for those concerned not only with environmental problems such as climate change and nuclear waste disposal, but also with emerging existential risks related to global pandemics and to forms of technological development such as biotechnology and artificial intelligence. The precautionary principle shifts the burden of proof onto those proposing technological developments to show how potential damage can be avoided. Entrenchment forces systematic consideration of potential risks to the well-being of future generations.

It is easy to understand why constitutions have been a particular focus for those who wish to safeguard the future. Constitutions set the ground rules for democracies. A constitution lays out the principles and values of a political community and the rules that shape the structure and practices of institutions. No higher political and legal status exists beyond entrenched constitutional provisions. Embedding constitutional provisions to safeguard and promote the interests of future generations promises a way of removing these issues from everyday politics: a structural protection against drivers of democratic myopia. The amendment of constitutions is, typically, more challenging than an ordinary statute. For example, an amendment may require super-majorities across chambers of bicameral systems or constitutional referendums. The enforcement of constitutional provisions typically rests with an independent constitutional court.

Constitutions can affect political decision-making in different ways.[20] First, constitutional provisions can constrain legislatures, governments, and other institutions where these fail to consider adequately the interests of future generations. Constitutions can be a brake on short-sighted behaviours. Decisions that depart from provisions are open to challenge through the constitutional courts. Second, in constitutional democracies, no stronger mechanism exists for signalling the significance of posterity. This is a polity's foundational text. Constitutions can play a substantial role in the shaping of collective beliefs, values, and action. The entrenchment of regard for future generations increases the likelihood that such regard becomes part and parcel of everyday political thinking. Third, constitutional courts bring an independent voice to bear in judgements about long-term interests. In principle, judges are not prey to the same pressures that push elected politicians towards short-term decision horizons. This autonomy varies from state to state, depending on the extent to which appointment procedures are politicised. Finally, the presence of constitutional provisions can play a role in reducing the uncertainty associated with long-term policy outcomes. Entrenchment signifies a degree of stability over time.

To what extent have constitutional provisions had a practical effect? Does the constitutionalisation of rights for future generations or of substantive long-term policy goals constrain the short-term imperatives that face decision makers? Future generations cannot represent their own interests in courts; in consequence the realisation of constitutional clauses relies on contemporary third parties. While many courts seem reticent to enforce constitutional clauses that defend the interests of future generations, successful cases have emerged.[21] For example, the Hague District Court granted the Urgenda Foundation, a civil society organisation, the right to represent the unborn. The court found that Dutch climate policies were harmful to present and future generations, and ordered greenhouse gas emissions to be reduced by at least 25 per cent by the end of 2020. In the Phillipines, the Supreme Court has established rules of procedure that allow any Filipino citizen to represent future generations. The willingness and capacity of civil society organisations such as Client Earth to make use of the court system to protect ecological well-being suggests that constitutional challenges are likely to be more prevalent. In some polities, for example in Hungary, independent agencies have been empowered to protect the constitutional rights of future generations, citizens being able to petition the body to take action through the courts. I will pick up this example in the next chapter.

Debates continue as to whether the constitutionalisation of limits on public debt has affected the economic policymaking of states.[22] The fiscal practices of countries such as Germany do appear to constrain debt by comparison to what happens in states without such constitutional provisions, although proponents argue that stronger provisions need to be in place. Critics of constitutionally prescribed debt ceilings are concerned that entrenching this fiscal principle may reduce the scope of long-term action. For example, debt created through investment in infrastructure, climate adaptation, and social policies with the explicit intention to protect and promote the interests of future generations could be judged unconstitutional. The danger is that one political perspective on the duties we owe to posterity may be constitutionalised to the detriment of alternative approaches.

To date, the impact of a constitutional approach to safeguarding the future has been relatively limited. The willingness of civil society organisations such as Client Earth and the Urgenda Foundation to take the fight for future generations into the court system suggests that this impact is likely to increase. One of the challenges faced by advocates, however, is the relatively vague and general specification of provisions. The more specific a constitutional provision is, the easier it is to enforce it. It can be difficult to make the case that a particular policy or development, just by itself, undermines the interests of future generations – typically, that is the cumulative effect of a series of activities. Ekeli argues for restricting the discussion of the rights of future generations to the 'basic physical and biological human needs necessary to survive and avoid serious and life-threatening diseases'.[23] Such a definition would encompass the right to protect the critical resources necessary for meeting those basic needs. This kind of appeal to basic needs and to the right to critical resources is a common strategy; but it faces at least two challenges. First, the specification of what constitutes basic needs and critical resources is not straightforward, and agreements do not go beyond a level of generality. Second, even this more parsimonious right cannot sidestep the cumulative nature of impacts, and hence the difficulty of using the courts to challenge specific policy developments.

So then, are constitutional provisions little more than window dressing? That would be too strong a judgement. The entrenchment of rights is not the end of the story – rather it is the beginning of a process. Once rights have been entrenched, the institutional machinery needs to be in place in order that these rights can be claimed effectively. The establishment and sustenance of that machinery is political. In the next chapter we will discuss the vulnerability of such machinery in the guise of the Hungarian Parliamentary Commissioner for Future Generations. At a minimum, to entrench constitutional provisions is a significant symbolic act – a recognition that the long-term interests of future generations need to be given due weight, legally and politically.

But what of the democratic legitimacy of a constitutional approach to safeguarding future generations? Constitutional remedies are celebrated because they put a break on the short-term activities of legislatures, governments, and administrations. This is why it is an attractive solution for moral and legal philosophers who seek to entrench principles of intergenerational justice in order to put them beyond the reach of democratic politics. Justice is given priority over democracy. Debates have long raged within democratic politics as to whether unelected judges, typically from privileged backgrounds, should be in a position to trump politicians elected by the people.[24] What should be the relative power of constitutional courts and legislatures? Similarly, should one generation be able to constrain the democratic decisions of future generations through the authoring of constitutional provisions that restrict their actions? Jefferson famously argued that, at the point where half of the people who established a constitution have died, the constitution must be revisited. It is no longer legitimate, since the majority of its authors are no longer present. This short book cannot do justice to the nuance of these debates. From a normative perspective, much depends on how easy it is for constitutional provisions to be revised – in other words, on the relationship between law and politics. In principle, constitutions are created through democratic processes and have amendment processes that allow them to be revisited. In some cases, the rules are so prohibitive that constitutional change is hard to imagine. This is the case in the United States. In his formulation of constitutional rights for future generations, Ekeli does not wish to empower courts to strike down laws or policies. Rather, in a manner reminiscent of his proposal for legislative reform, the constitutional court would be empowered to require impact assessments, to delay adoption until after an election, or to require a binding referendum.[25]

The balance of powers between elected legislatures and constitutional courts needs to be carefully considered. The legitimacy of arrangements will be affected by the powers afforded to courts, by how judges are selected, and by the manner in which constitutions can be amended. The constitutional protection of future generations indicates the seriousness with which democratic polities consider their interests. Entrenchment is a recognition that these interests should not be discounted in decision-making.

Conclusion

The title of this chapter is 'Reimagining Established Institutions'. Plenty of reimagining is going on. Design proposals abound. Most remain on the drawing table, being often limited by their political feasibility and the extent to which they may undermine long-established democratic principles

– for example, principles of universal suffrage and equal representation. Actual restructuring in the name of future generations is relatively limited. We can point to institutional developments such as the Finnish Parliamentary Committee for the Future, or to constitutional provisions that have been tested in court. Such practices remain very much at the margins of democratic politics.

The focus on the very different institutions of legislatures and constitutions exposes at least three challenges for democratic design. The first is how to build legitimacy, in particular trust and confidence that institutions will consistently promote, over time, the interests of the unborn. The second relates to the social position of decision makers who are empowered to make judgements in the interests of future generations. Most of the proposals in this chapter focus on empowering political representatives or judges. The people who play these roles are hardly the most diverse social group, which means that conceptions of the future are likely to be limited. The third challenge is a tension that emerges between independence and diversity. The independence of constitutional courts is valuable in that it protects the institution from drivers of short-termism such as electoral cycles and partisan interests. By comparison, legislatures are more likely to be constituted by a relatively more diverse body of members who, at least in principle, can bring different perspectives to bear on what we owe posterity. Independence and diversity may pull the democratic designer in different directions. A democratic politics for future generations needs to take questions of legitimacy, independence, and diversity seriously.

3

Bringing in an
Independent Voice

We should not be surprised that simply reworking the structure and practices of the established institutions of democracies is inadequate for dealing with the challenges of long-term decision-making. These are institutions that propagate democratic myopia, hence a few design tweaks are unlikely to have significant impact on their established dynamics. We need to look further afield. This chapter investigates the potential of independent institutions that are designed with the specific purpose of protecting and defending the interests of future generations and of embedding more long-term thinking into democratic systems. The combination of purpose and independence from partisan and electoral politics potentially creates a locus of power within the political system that is more immune to the drivers of short-termism. Consistency in action on the part of independent bodies offers the potential to hold governments to their commitments across time.

Governments and legislatures have a long history of creating independent bodies in the governance of particular areas of policy. The Committee for Climate Change (CCC) in the United Kingdom is an especially relevant development, with an independent role, established by legislation, in overseeing government mitigation and adaptation policy. We find similar agencies created to protect and promote, for example, the interests of children and the environment; and they have clear and obvious long-term motivations. A qualitatively different type of independent institution – offices for future generations (OFGs) – has emerged in a small number of democratic polities.

This chapter begins with brief reflections on the CCC before concentrating on three OFGs – in Hungary, in Israel, and in Wales. The three institutions vary in their powers and in their location within the democratic ecology of each country. The story of these OFGs indicates the challenges that designing institutions to safeguard posterity face. The Israeli body has been abolished. The powers of the Hungarian body are diminished. The Welsh body, a relatively recent creation, is the only one that remains standing in its original form. I will consider what conditions need to be in place for OFGs to thrive.[1]

The Committee for Climate Change

The CCC in the United Kingdom is an example of an independent body with a particular future-related task.[2] This committee was established as part of the innovative 2008 Climate Change Act, the world's first national legislation that enshrines legal targets for carbon reduction. The initial target within the legislation was to achieve 80 per cent decarbonisation by 2050; more recently, the figure was revised to net zero carbon emissions by 2050. This is an unconditional target: it does not rely on other countries taking action. The role of the CCC is to advise on progress on mitigation and adaptation, in particular to formulate and assess the realisation of five-year carbon budgets. The CCC publishes annual reports on government progress.

The CCC is a positive development in that it ensures transparency of government action and has had a noticeable effect, being able at times to hold a reluctant government to account against self-imposed targets. It has challenged the government as to whether it has the policies in place to achieve its net zero target.[3] The presence and activities of the CCC improve public confidence in the continuity of government action over time in this critical and long-term policy domain. The same logic extends across a range of kindred domains: it has led for example to the creation of the National Infrastructure Commission (NIC) in the United Kingdom.[4] We are witnessing the incremental establishment of independent bodies, each with discrete responsibilities for aspects of long-term policymaking and delivery. This strategy has two limitations. First, it can generate coordination issues: there is potential overlap and tensions between the activities of independent agencies charged with different policy mandates – for example, between the CCC's responsibilities for adaptation and the activities of the NIC, which has a broader remit than ensuring carbon reduction and climate adaptation. Second, the extent of these bodies' influence across government is limited. The role of the CCC is to ensure progress towards the 2050 target. Making the case for an earlier decarbonisation date to combat the climate emergency is outside its mandate.

While recognising the importance of agencies such as the CCC in their particular policy domain,

61

independent OFGs offer a more synoptic intervention, promoting long-term thinking across all relevant areas of public authority. Only a few examples of such OFGs exist, but there is much that can be learned from their different structures and practices – and from their fate.

Israel

The Commission for Future Generations was established in Israel in 2001 but lasted only for one parliamentary term, until 2006. The commission's work was focused predominantly on the Knesset, the Israeli parliament. The commissioner, Shlomo Shoham, had extensive rights to obtain information, examine parliamentary bills and secondary legislation, and request reasonable time to prepare opinions on proposed legislation where he judged that there was potential harm to future generations. The power to request time was particularly significant because it gave the commission the capacity to delay legislation. The commission could engage on any subject on the parliament's agenda apart from defence and foreign affairs.

Ironically, an institution created by parliament in recognition of its own shortcomings was abolished also by the parliament, because its influence was being felt by elected politicians. Shoham argues: 'The more the Commission's voice was heard, the more the criticism increased.'[5] A Knesset Research and Information Center review suggests that members of the Knesset raised two primary objections that led to the commission's annulment: the commission's operational costs and the extent of its authority to interfere in their work.[6] The short-term interests of parliamentarians quickly trumped long-term considerations. Shoham reports that he was also challenged about how he could speak on behalf of future generations:

> I have been asked – more than once – if we have the authority to make any kind of decision for future generations, and if so, where it comes from … How do I allow myself to speak in the name of those who have not yet been born? How do I decide what policy is good or appropriate for them and what is not?[7]

At the end of its first full term of office in 2006, the commission was not replaced and a bill of annulment for the institution was brought to the Knesset. Once an institution to defend the interests of future generations was created, its right to speak on their behalf and to delay the law-making function of parliament was brought into question.

Hungary

The Hungarian Parliamentary Commissioner for Future Generations was established in 2007 and lasted for four years in its original form. The primary function of the commissioner was to act as an ombudsman. The Hungarian constitution establishes that the state as a whole and every person in it are obliged to protect, sustain, and preserve the environment for future generations. The commissioner was empowered to conduct investigations on citizens' complaints and to appeal to the Constitutional Court or the Curia of Hungary (supreme court) in cases where national or local legislation may be in violation of the country's constitution. The commissioner had the power to suspend administrative actions that it perceived to be in violation of the constitution. For both philosophical and practical reasons, the first commissioner, Sándor Fülöp, never actually used this power. He was concerned that doing so would change the role of the commissioner from being an oversight body to being one that engaged in governing duties. The relative lack of resources meant that such action would be hard to sustain.[8]

As in Israel, here too the independent OFG found itself at odds with members of the political class: in this case, with the right-wing Fedesz government. By adopting a new constitution in 2011, the government aimed to eradicate many of the state's checks and balances. Agencies with independent powers were particular targets. The commissioner was vulnerable also because the OFG found itself in conflict, in high-profile actions, with financially significant supporters of the governing regime. To most commentators' surprise, the commissioner had a partial stay of execution, as the institution morphed into the Deputy Ombudsman for Future Generations. The new ombudsman works under the country's General Ombudsman. In its new form, the body has no rights of investigation or opinion without the agreement of the General Ombudsman and has been shorn of resources.[9] The government's partial change of mind appears to have been driven by a highly political reinterpretation, in explicitly nationalist terms, of the notion of protecting future generations and the environment: in this reinterpretation, 'future generations' means future generations of the Hungarian people.

The Israeli and Hungarian OFGs operated differently. The Israeli commission was a creature of parliament – it focused primarily on scrutinising legislative activity. By contrast, the Hungarian commissioner acted primarily as an ombudsman, drawing authority to act from the constitution and taking on complaints from the public. Both bodies faced the same challenge. As soon as the institutions started to bite – to restrict the government's and parliamentarians' room for manoeuvre – their powers were removed or reduced. These are stark reminders of the way in which short-term interests can trump long-term governance arrangements.

Wales

The Future Generations Commissioner for Wales is a more recent development, established in 2016 under the Well-Being of Future Generations (Wales) Act of the previous year.[10] The first holder of that role is Sophie Howe. Sustainable development is a core principle in the UK act of parliament that devolved powers to the Welsh Assembly in 1999. The Well-Being of Future Generations Act is the legislative realisation of this principle. The Act places a duty on all government ministries, public authorities, and public service boards to consider future generations in their activities. It lays out a sustainable development principle, a set of well-being goals, and five 'ways of working' that public authorities are expected to embody in their decision-making: the long term, prevention, integration, collaboration, and involvement. Ministries as well as public bodies and boards are required to set relevant well-being objectives, in line with the principle and the goals defined by the Act. The commissioner's role is to support the activities and actions of public bodies and to monitor and assess the extent to which these bodies realise their objectives. The commissioner is also empowered to publish, one year before assembly elections, a Future Generations report that contains an assessment of the improvements public bodies need to make.

Compared to the commissioners in Hungary and Israel, the Welsh commissioner does not have equivalent parliamentary rights and powers: the focus of this OFG is on the actions of the executive (the Welsh government) and the 43 other public bodies and public service boards in Wales. It is too early to say whether the commissioner's office will have consistent and meaningful effect over time. The public position of Sophie Howe in the long-standing debate over the widening of a major highway appears to have been influential in the Welsh government's recent decision to abandon the scheme on the grounds that this was not a long-term solution to transport problems.[11] If the commissioner is able to exert influence on long-established policy tropes such as the need to increase road capacity, then the potential of the OFG to realise more sustained attention on the interests of future generations is promising. The Welsh experience is having influence beyond its borders. Gibraltar has recently established legislation to create a similar framework and a campaign is underway in the United Kingdom to establish analogous arrangements, although with more extensive powers for the commissioner.

Beyond national bodies, proposals have emerged for transnational or global OFGs. Ideas such as of a European-level OFG, or of a global United Nations body, have been serious subjects of consideration within the relevant policy communities.[12] Independent bodies do not need to be tied to nation states and could bring a much needed voice and scrutiny on behalf of future generations into transnational governance, especially where these bodies are afforded powers in relation to relevant international court systems.

The promise of OFGs

The promise of OFGs is that they bring a consistent, independent, and impartial voice into the political system – a voice that aims to safeguard the future. They do not suffer electoral pressures and their independence provides distance from powerful social interests. Their presence can ameliorate some of the uncertainty and lack of confidence about long-term policies. OFGs can be trusted to continue the promotion of the long term over time – and, importantly, across changes in government.

The dissolution of the Israeli Commission and the downgrading of its Hungarian counterpart cast doubt on the robustness and perceived legitimacy of OFGs. In both cases, the very existence of these institutions was brought into question by elected politicians. One reading is that these two OFGs were simply given too much power, namely the power to delay legislation (Israel) and to bring cases to court (Hungary). This is part of the explanation as to why the powers of the Welsh Commissioner are more subscribed. Care is needed in interpreting the fate of these bodies solely in terms of their powers. At least in part, their fate can be explained by particular sets of political circumstances. In Israel, it appears that the commissioner's style and approach were not appreciated by many parliamentarians, and especially by more orthodox religious leaders, who felt that the office was pushing a secular agenda. In Hungary, the commissioner was not singled out – rather the right-wing government removed a whole series of independent scrutiny bodies as part of its broader political project. Part of the function of the commissioner was maintained, albeit with less reach, which is more than can be said for many other independent bodies that were vanquished completely.

Powers such as legislative and administrative delay, or the ability to bring cases to court, are desirable in that they strengthen the capacity of OFGs to act so as to safeguard future generations. However, they raise questions of democratic legitimacy: should non-elected bodies intervene in the political process to halt the actions of elected representatives? The charge is that independent bodies are unaccountable. Their presence and actions undermine democratic principles. This is to misunderstand the political and legal status of such agencies. Independent bodies have a long democratic pedigree. Precursors to the current practice have been traced back to overseers, auditors, and supervisors in classical Athens.[13] While these institutions were very different from OFGs (in both ancient and contemporary democracies), independent bodies have been created in recognition of the fact that democracies display dysfunctionalities of different kinds and require appropriate institutional remedies. In the case of OFGs, this is a recognition of the tendency of democratic institutions towards harmful short-termism, where the effects of current policy on future generations are not given due weight.

It is often forgotten, in the criticism of independent status and power, that such features have been granted by law. The bodies that received them are the creation of legislatures. Their powers and legitimacy are bestowed by elected politicians. Hence they can be held accountable by the legislature and their powers can be revoked, as the examples of Israel and Hungary demonstrate.

The criticism of OFGs resonates to some extent with that of constitutional courts noted in the previous chapter. No OFG has yet been afforded constitutional status and powers, although the capacity to delay legislative and administrative action and to submit cases for court action is far from insignificant. Where constitutional protection for OFGs is suggested,[14] these bodies would still be subject to removal, but typically the legislature would need to have a higher threshold for

71

action. Having it could have been an extra layer of protection in Israel and Hungary. Whatever the threshold, it is the capacity of the legislature to both create and revoke the powers of independent agencies that distinguishes such institutions from anti-democratic ones, such as guardians beyond the control of democratic politics.[15]

Even if a strong case can be made for the existence of OFGs and for ensuring that they have the capacity to act effectively, we are left with two challenges. The first is that they are politically vulnerable. The second is that they may not be able to make sound judgements about the interests of future generations.

The Hungarian and Israeli Commissioners lasted for one full term only before they were reorganised or annulled. The fate of these two OFGs creates a significant dilemma. These oversight bodies are instituted by politicians, in recognition of the structural tendency to favour the short term over the long term. The self-same politicians, when they find themselves frustrated by the activities of the oversight bodies they instituted, abolish them at relatively low political cost. Institutions designed to challenge short-termism become victims of short-term politics themselves. Reflecting on the fate of the Israeli OFG, Jonathan Boston notes:

The early demise of the Commission offers a number of salutary lessons for policy-makers in other advanced democracies who might contemplate creating a similar kind of institution. Above all, it suggests that a statutory basis, a physical location in the heart of a country's main representative institution, and significant rights of access to information and to key decision-makers, although obviously helpful conditions, are not sufficient for success.[16]

Compared to most other independent agencies, OFGs are especially vulnerable politically because they lack a strong constituency that will offer political support when they are threatened. Most independent agencies have politically influential lobby groups that provide political capital, placing a brake on government action, should the government wish to ignore or even abolish the body. As Boston argues, an OFG 'runs the risk of having few friends and defenders. At the same time, it is bound to generate enemies.'[17] Vested interests within and beyond government and parliament will not take kindly to bodies that disrupt established patterns of influence and material advantage in the name of long-term governance. The challenge is to create a political and institutional context within which an OFG is able to defend itself against the very short-term dynamics that it is established to confront. Otherwise its position will remain precarious.

Constitutional protection is one possible solution. This is a step beyond the constitutional developments I discussed in the last chapter. Just as the rights of future generations are increasingly entrenched in constitutional provisions, so too would be the existence and powers of an OFG.[18] Other strategies are needed until this becomes an established route of institutionalisation.

OFGs *and the participation agenda*

Elements of the practice of the Hungarian and Welsh OFGs offer one route to enhancing the political robustness of these institutions, namely public participation. The Hungarian Commissioner's ombudsman function is one strategy. The public's capacity to make representations to the commissioner acts as a mechanism for building public credibility and support. While one term was not enough to establish the degree of public support necessary for defending the institution against reform in Hungary, ombudsmen have emerged as significant political actors historically. As Ludvig

Beckman and Fredrik Uggla argue, in a number of cases 'ombudsmen have managed to become politically important actors and effective defenders of citizens' rights even when they may have been created primarily as symbols, and in spite of the difficulty of promoting sensitive issues in a generally unfavourable context'.[19] Their capacity to act as trusted representatives of citizens has often helped them to achieve political prominence.

In his position as Hungarian Commissioner, Fülöp actively championed a broader participation agenda beyond his ombudsman function. As an environmental lawyer, he drew particular inspiration from the Aarhus Convention, formally known as the Convention on Access to Information, Public Participation in Decision-Making and Access to Justice in Environmental Matters of the United Nations Economic Commission for Europe (UNECE). Adopted in 1998 in the Danish City of Aarhus, this groundbreaking Convention establishes a range of individual substantive and procedural rights in environmental decision-making.[20] Fülöp consistently argues that the realisation of the constitutional right to a healthy environment requires special attention to rights to environmental information and public participation.[21]

The Welsh case is explicitly tied to public participation both in the creation of the Well-Being of Future Generations (Wales) Act and in the working practices of the commissioner's office itself. The national conversation 'The Wales We Want' helped to shape the Act, as it engaged with communities, civil society organisations, and others across the nation. One of the seven foundations for the well-being of future generations within the Act that were established through this consultation process states that 'greater engagement in the democratic process, a stronger citizen voice and active participation in decision-making is fundamental for the well-being of future generations'.[22] One of the five ways in which public authorities should work, according to the Act, is through 'involvement'. Thus the function of Commissioner for Future Generations not only was constituted through a participatory process, but is expected to promote citizen participation across public bodies in Wales and to embed participation as a fundamental element of its own working practices.

To a degree, the commissioner has embraced this participatory ethos. Howe employed an active public participation strategy in the consultation process for the *Strategic Plan 2017–2023*,[23] engaging 1,300 people via an online tool, workshops, and face-to-face conversation sessions. While these are fairly traditional modes of consultation, the process broadens the perspectives that inform the commissioner's priorities and programme of work and at the same time raises the profile of the body among the public. An explicit commitment exists within the *Strategic Plan* to '[c]hampion effective public involvement and engagement, challenging ourselves and others to better understand the needs of our communities, our people and their influence on the decisions that affect them'.[24] The language is promising. How this goal will be realised in practice is yet to be seen.

The way in which the Welsh Commissioner has begun to reach out to communities and other stakeholders to develop priorities suggests the potential for more extensive embedding of public participation in the workings of an OFG. It is the logical extension of the commissioner's commitment to '[w]alk the talk – challenging our team to be the change we want to see in others'.[25] This points to an alternative source of democratic legitimacy beyond statute: a form of 'downward accountability' direct from agency to citizens.[26] Independent agencies can develop strategies of responsiveness to citizens as much as legislatures and executives. Building a strong relationship directly with citizens reduces the scope of any action designed to ignore or remove independent agencies.

Participation also offers an answer to the second challenge faced by OFGs. How can they speak for future generations? This was the explicit challenge faced by the Israeli Commissioner, but is a recurring issue for any institution that claims to act as a surrogate for, or representative of, the unborn. Legislatures embody a variety of perspectives on the interests of future generations, given the plurality of representatives, although they are constrained by electoral-party motivations and by the limited range of social backgrounds from which the political class is drawn. For commissioners, judgements rest with individuals. The worry here is that the judgement of a commissioner for future generations would be partial. This could be read as a concern that individual commissioners would use their position to advance their own interests in the name of future generations. Even if we do not have reason to suspect the motives of a commissioner, judgements will be limited by the lack of diversity of social perspectives.

Shoham, the Israeli Commissioner, argues that he was pushing no single vision of the future, but rather 'sought to ensure that future generations would have the *broadest spectrum of choices possible*'.[27]

He suggests that sustainable development 'provides a systematic rule, or measurement of action that needs to be carried out in the present time in order to do justice to future generations – leaving them the space for choice'.[28] This is meant to circumvent the very political battles that rage over what sustainable development means in practice and what the boundaries of the 'space for choice' should look like, particularly where different interpretations, religious and other, of the good life are in play. Any 'systematic rule' operates only in fairly abstract terms. A similar problem exists for those who argue that judgements of commissioners should focus on the realisation of basic needs and critical resources across generations. As I argued in the discussion of constitutional provisions in the previous chapter, in practice this apparently simple formulation not only requires agreement on what constitutes basic needs and critical resources, but also provides no guidance on how to manage the distributional challenges that arise within and across generations when we are faced with competing policy options.

A second response to the concern of a single commissioner having the power to make judgements is to draw on the tradition of collegial panels in France – commissioners as opposed to a single commissioner – or on the US practice of bipartisan commissions.[29] This was the practice of the now defunct Sustainable Development Commission in the United Kingdom. A number of commissioners with different specialisms were brought together to act as a corporate body. This certainly expands the range of perspectives that are brought to bear on judgements about the interests of the unborn, although membership of such offices is likely to remain relatively restricted to those with particular political allegiances or technical forms of expertise. Social diversity is lacking. Anja Karnein offers a variation on this approach. If we recognise that different generations may have different interests, then we can pluralise representation by employing several commissioners who represent different aspects of the future.[30]

Enhancing participation in the work of OFGs offers a potential solution. Participation can bring a diversity of perspectives. We can see this logic at work in the practice of the Hungarian Commissioner. Fülöp argues that 'we did not want to project our own vision. With over 200 substantive complaints per year, there was no need to invent new problems.'[31] A complaints system ensures a degree of responsiveness to public concerns, although communities have differential capacities to take such action. Public participation is a key component of the legislative framework within which the Welsh Commissioner operates and engagement strategies should become the norm, as part of the working practices of the OFG and other public bodies.

Conclusion

OFGs provide an innovative vehicle for the representation of future generations within democratic systems. Debate continues as to how much power such independent offices should hold. The fate of the Hungarian and Israeli OFGs suggests caution. The Welsh approach is more focused on persuasion and has limited formal powers to enforce action on public bodies. Without significant power to affect change, it is not clear how effective such OFGs can be in acting as a brake on short-termism.

Given the failures of parliaments and governments to act in the long term, OFGs could well be a critical actor in changing democratic dynamics and in challenging democratic dysfunctionalities. They will be vulnerable institutions when coming face to face with powerful interests that challenge their ability to speak on behalf of those yet unborn.

Can Democracy Safeguard the Future?

The suggestion in this chapter is that the participatory practices of the Hungarian and Welsh Commissioners offer the basis of a solution to the legitimacy challenges that OFGs face. Participation should not be just about strengthening the position of OFGs; it should be also a way of bringing plural voices into political judgements of how to safeguard the future. As the final chapter will argue, participation can be understood as central to a broader strategy of enriching democracy for future generations.

4

Deepening Democracy for the Long Term

Participatory democracy would appear to be a counterintuitive approach to long-term governance. The short-sightedness of the public is widely viewed as a fundamental determinant of democratic myopia. However, as I argued in the first chapter, this is an oversimplification. The public's perspectives on future generations are highly structured by the context in which they are articulated. A long-term perspective is rarely taken by people when they make immediate and everyday decisions – with the exception of those motivated by 'lifetime-transcending interests'.[1] But everyday decision-making is a very different context from the kind of engagement that is structured to orient participants explicitly towards consideration of the future.

What is it, then, that participation can offer to long-term democratic governance? How can participatory democracy counter short-termism? First, participation can enable more inclusive judgements about the interests of future generations. Second, it can enhance the perceived legitimacy of political decision-making for the long term. And, third, it can foster a practice of democracy that is worth passing on to future generations.

A participatory politics for future generations recognises the limitations of most of the proposals for long-term governance that we have discussed in this book. These tend to have strong elitist and technocratic tendencies: they tend to restructure or create institutions that empower members of the established political class to safeguard future generations. Such approaches fail to engender inclusive judgements, fail to bolster the legitimacy of long-term governance, and fail to rejuvenate the practice of democracy. When we are faced with the dysfunctionalities of democratic myopia, a more radical solution is needed. A significant part of this solution is to embed forms of participatory and deliberative democracy in our political practices and structures.

The potential for public participation to bring to bear a diversity of voices and perspectives on the interests of future generations offers a creative response to the temporal plurality problem – the recognition that long-term policy requires us to balance different interests across and within generations. Since the unborn cannot be present to articulate their own interests, we require a second-best solution. Drawing on feminist insights, a second-best solution is to recognise that social groups would offer different perspectives on the interests of future generations that reflect diverse social, political, economic, and environmental experiences and identities. They would be sensitive to different vulnerabilities within and across generations. The widest possible participation of social groups – especially those whose voices are often not heard – would ensure that public judgements are informed by a diversity of perspectives on what those different future interests may entail. It would allow us to understand where agreement and divergence exist across social groups. This is not to discount the importance of scientific and legal expertise. Rather it is to recognise that richer judgements, which reflect more accurately the pluralistic character and interests of future generations, would emerge as a result of public participation strategies that engage with and across diverse communities. Otherwise judgements will simply reflect the limited perspectives of those who already exercise power, most probably reproducing existing imbalances of power across generations.

Second, participatory politics offers a way of legitimising difficult decisions. At the moment, critical decisions are being taken – or often not taken – by socially and politically remote institutions that are regarded by the public as out of touch and unresponsive. Distrust of established political institutions and representatives is a driver of uncertainty when it comes to long-term decision-making. The danger is that the proposed institutional designs discussed so far in this book will continue to reinforce this social and political distance. A participatory strategy promises decisions that better reflect the lived experiences, aspirations and concerns of communities. A participatory politics responds to the lack of a constituency for future generations. Through participation, such a constituency can be built, so that it may challenge short-term electoral motivations and the influence of vested interests.

Finally and relatedly, embedding a participatory politics in our democratic institutions will help people to realise obligations to future generations. If the maxim is that we should pass on to those who follow us a set of social and natural goods that are at least as robust as our own, then democratic practices are one element of realising that duty. As Dennis Thompson argues, our minimal duty is 'to seek to preserve a democratic process that gives future citizens at least as much capacity for collective decision-making as present citizens have'.[2] He adds:

> If we believe that the control that citizens now enjoy is inadequate, we may wish to adopt a more demanding version of the principle. It would stipulate that any current political generation should seek, up to the point that control over their own decision-making begins to decrease, to maximize the control that future generations will enjoy.[3]

Here is an opportunity to pass on something more valuable to our descendants. Democratic culture has been deteriorating in recent years, with less and less investment in democratic infrastructure and practices. A politics that is sensitive to the perspectives of, and empowers, diverse communities is the essence of democracy itself. What could be more valuable to future generations than a participatory politics that deals effectively with long-term challenges? What more can we offer than the governing capacity to make hard decisions in a way that realises democratic principles?

Such a participatory politics can be pragmatic in character or more radical. A pragmatic politics looks to embed participation in the decision-making processes of existing democratic institutions. For example, it would bolster the legitimacy of offices for future generations (OFGs) by enhancing both the inclusiveness of their judgements and their political standing in the eyes of politicians and the public. This is the argument of the previous chapter: an OFG that engages with and draws support from diverse communities makes for more inclusive decision-making and is harder to ignore. A pragmatic participatory strategy can democratise elite and technocratic institutions, both the ones that exist and the ones that are being proposed.

A more radical deepening of democracy can also be envisioned – one in which participatory institutions are empowered to make decisions in their own right. This may seem like an improbable, perhaps impossible dream – or, for some, a nightmare! The seeds of this more radical orientation are already present in current practice and social demands.

The participatory turn has found support in mainstream political developments. Participation is one of the key principles of sustainable development as articulated by the United Nations and other international bodies. In 1992, the landmark Rio Earth

Summit agreed on Agenda 21, which makes the case for systematic public engagement, particularly with vulnerable communities. The Aarhus Convention, referred to in the previous chapter, establishes a range of procedural rights in environmental decision-making. The UN Sustainable Development Goals call for the adoption of responsive, inclusive and participatory decision-making if the goals are to be realised and sustained. The Well-Being of Future Generations (Wales) Act, also discussed in the previous chapter, defines public involvement as one of the five ways of working expected by the Future Generations Commissioner and by the public bodies subject to the Act. The time is ripe for calls for participation to move beyond minority preoccupation and become a fundamental organising principle of long-term governance.

Designing participation for the long term

Participatory democracy for future generations does not assume that any kind of participation will promote long-term thinking. Many participatory processes are explicitly designed to respond to more immediate needs – especially of more vulnerable and marginalised communities. The much celebrated participatory budgeting that spread across Brazil and beyond is a useful example. The intention behind this participatory institution is to invert investment priorities in the name of social justice, budgets becoming more responsive to the needs of poorer communities. The annual round of investments in Brazilian participatory budgets has often generated important investments for the long term – for example the building of critical infrastructure such as roads and sanitation facilities in poor neighbourhoods. However, the annual nature of the available spend is less hospitable to long-term developments, which often need recurring and sustained funding. Participatory budgets have been less successful in mobilising poorer communities to participate in more strategic policy developments. Such forums tend to attract those who already are politically engaged and organized.[4]

What, then, do we know about participatory design for the long term? What design features of participatory process promote a long-term orientation?

A good place to start is the work of the Nobel economist Elinor Ostrom. She spent much of her career developing insights into how resources are best managed for the long term. Her answer was to empower local communities.[5] By giving communities direct control over the resources in their locality, the tragedy of the commons – the overuse of non-renewable resources to the detriment of public goods – can be overcome. Ostrom's work focuses on direct control of resources by the local community, although in her later work she reflects on the capacities of higher levels of governance. The argument for empowerment remains the same: meaningful control exercised by the affected communities over matters that have direct impact on their lives.

Ostrom argues that such control needs to be exercised through inclusive communication among the participants. Better judgements emerge from hearing and reflecting on different forms of knowledge. The tendency is for specialist expertise and for the perspectives of established political actors to dominate. For Ostrom, these perspectives are partial and fail to reflect the lived experiential knowledge that accumulates within communities.

While she did not use the term, Ostrom's ideas prefigure work on deliberative democracy that rests on the principle that, for any decision to be legitimate, it must be made through a process of free and fair deliberation among equals. Such inclusive decision-making is likely to be morally and epistemically more robust, since it draws on plural and diverse forms of knowledge and insights. Claus Offe and Ulrich Preuss argue that deliberation is not only fact-regarding and other-regarding, but also *future-regarding*.[6] Michael McKenzie suggests a number of mechanisms that come into play to orient deliberation towards the long term and to make us consider the interests of future generations.[7] First, from a psychological angle, deliberation activates our system 2 reasoning, that is, our 'slow' thinking. Recalling the distinction introduced in the first chapter, deliberation encourages participants to move from the rather automatic and reactive system 1 orientation and motivates them to adopt a reflective and considered mode of judgement. Second, deliberation requires mutual justification. With this condition in place, it is hard to defend publicly short-term and self-serving preferences. Through the act of orienting participants towards the common good, the interests of future generations become a subject of moral concern, to be considered and balanced against other demands within the deliberative process. Third, deliberation enables coordination. Responding to long-term challenges requires not only difficult decisions but also compliance from institutions and the broader population. Deliberation can empower the identification and achievement of shared goals and objectives. It creates a space in which credible commitments can be articulated, tested, and maintained over time. MacKenzie takes one step further, suggesting that deliberation can also promote coordination across generations. We cannot engage in mutual justification with future generations. However, through deliberation, the justification for our current actions will be transparent to those who follow. For Mackenzie, this transparency is an important condition for promoting compliance and coordination between parties separated across time.

The promise of deliberative mini-publics

Designing participatory governance to safeguard the future suggests a combination of empowerment, inclusiveness, and deliberation. What might this look like in practice?

Deliberative mini-publics (DMPs) are one set of participatory designs that potentially fulfils these criteria and is garnering a great deal of attention at present. This is not to say such bodies are the only, or a superior, form of participatory governance for the long term. DMPs are not a democratic panacea. Rather the combination of design characteristics and actual practice makes them worthy of sustained consideration.

DMPs are participatory institutions in which randomly selected citizens learn, reflect, and deliberate on often complex and controversial areas of public policy before they come to make recommendations. DMPs are carefully designed to ensure that the diverse body of participants is exposed to a range of witnesses with different forms of knowledge and insights on the issue at hand and has space and time to work its way through the complexities of issues. Examples of DMPs are citizens' assemblies, citizens' juries, consensus conferences, deliberative polls, planning cells.[8]

DMPs have been commissioned to take on a wide range of tasks, and a number of these have, explicitly, long-term horizons. Consensus conferences originally developed by the Danish Board of Technology have provided recommendations on emerging scientific and technological developments, in areas such as artificial intelligence (AI) and the use of transgenic animals. Citizens' juries and panels have been established on urban, transport, and other forms of planning in Canada, Australia, and beyond. Two select committees in the UK parliament employed a citizens' assembly, in an attempt to break the political deadlock on the future of social care funding.[9] Deliberative polls on energy provision in Texas provided evidence of informed public support for renewable energy and energy conservation that helped to reshape utility energy provision in the state.[10] Experiments with citizens' juries in Australia, Canada, and the United States, as well as the international World Wide Views project, indicate the potential of these bodies to consider aspects of climate change.[11] The direct action movement Extinction Rebellion has raised the stakes with its demand for a national citizens' assembly in the United Kingdom on the climate and ecological emergency. While the quality of initiatives has been variable, the number of local authorities that have established citizens' assemblies and other deliberative processes on the climate emergency, or have committed to them, gives an indication of the resonance of this demand. The decision by President Macron and six House of Commons select committees to commission respectively the Citizens' Convention on Climate Change and the UK Climate Assembly reveals the extent to which the model has gained political traction at the national level.[12]

More systematic analysis of the temporal orientation of DMPs is needed. The evidence we have suggests that, when well organised and resourced, given a clear task and adequate time to respond effectively, they outperform more traditional democratic institutions in the way in which they orient participants towards considering long-term implications, often on issues where public and political preferences are not well formed.[13]

It is the unusual combination of random selection and facilitated deliberation that sets apart the various DMPs when it comes to their potential to ameliorate significant aspects of democratic myopia. Random selection plays two functions. First, it generates a socially and cognitively diverse group. Apart from deliberative polls (which bring together hundreds of participants to deliberate over a weekend), most DMPs apply quota sampling to ensure that the selected body broadly reflects the social and cognitive diversity of the population. Common quotas include demographic character-istics such as gender, ethnicity, age, education, social class, and, for some designs, salient political attitudes. For example, the UK Climate Assembly ensured that participants mirrored the attitudes towards climate change in the wider population. Minority groups are at times over-sampled, a measure designed to ensure a larger presence within the body. This increases the likelihood that disempowered voices are heard and considered and builds confidence among politically marginalised groups to articulate their perspectives. The in-built diversity of DMPs is critical if we want to ensure that a variety of perspectives, drawn from different social positions within society, are present among participants. DMPs are arguably the most socially and cognitively diverse of all democratic institutions in contemporary polities. This ensures that a diversity of perspectives on the interests of future generations are brought to bear in their deliberations and decision-making processes.

The second function of random selection recalls ancient Athenian democracy, where sortition (along with rapid rotation) provided a defence against asymmetries in social and economic power.[14] Sortition – selection by lot – was introduced in classical Athens as a bulwark against powerful warring families. Given that one of the drivers for short-termism is the power of entrenched interests, a DMP creates a space in which participants are relatively protected from their influence and actions. Random selection is a protection against strategic action from those with structural power who benefit from the current social and economic arrangements that privilege the short term.

The combination of diversity and protection from strategic action that sortition enables is a critical condition for realising democratic deliberation.

But deliberation does not occur naturally. This is particularly the case for the heterogenous groups of people with very different social perspectives brought together in DMPs. A critical factor is that DMPs are facilitated spaces. Facilitation ensures fairness and equality as participants learn about the issue at hand, hear from and question a cross-section of witnesses, reflect on what they have heard and listen to the views of other participants. Facilitation promotes equality of voice and respectful interactions across a diverse group that differs significantly in terms of confidence, experience, and interests. DMPs approximate the type of communicative rather than strategic motivation celebrated by deliberative democrats. Participants are given the time and space to reflect on the long-term consequences of social choices as they become informed by the variety of perspectives offered by fellow participants and witnesses.

Random selection and facilitated deliberation are underpinned by independence. Typically commissioned by public authorities, DMPs are generally organised and facilitated by independent bodies. This is an insurance against co-option. Embodying random selection, facilitated deliberation and independence, DMPs are well placed to counter drivers of democratic myopia. The diversity of perspectives promises increased sensitivity towards the diversity of interests among and across future generations. Sortition embodies a different democratic logic, which protects participants from the short-term determinants of electoral, party, and interest group politics. DMPs remove participants from everyday practices that structure thought and action and place into an independent space that encourages collective consideration of obligations to future generations.

Critical voices

DMPs have their critics. It would not be an innovation if it did not generate reproach. Criticisms take a number of forms. The first is a strong scepticism that everyday citizens have the cognitive capacity to undertake such challenging tasks. True, citizens do not become technical experts in the topics they engage with. That is also the case for politicians. The issue is whether they are informed enough and have enough time to come to sound judgements. The design of DMPs ensures that participants hear and question witnesses with different perspectives on the issue at hand. The diversity and the informed deliberation they embody give them an advantage over established political institutions. It is striking how often sceptical politicians and expert witnesses become advocates when they have attended DMPs and observed their deliberations.

A second set of criticisms challenge the use of sortition. Sortition is taken to lack legitimacy because it undermines democratic accountability. Now, sortition certainly challenges the traditional way in which we understand accountability: the absence of elections means that the general public does not get to authorise the selected partici-pants. But this line of criticism too quickly equates democracy with elections. It too quickly overlooks the democratic heritage of sortition. Sortition rests on a different form of democratic legitimacy. The principle is that anyone has the right and capacity to be selected and to be part of the collective that makes political judgements on behalf of the polity. Electoral accountability is replaced by deliberative accountability: randomly selected participants give a public account of their recommendations and of how they were generated.

DMPs are also challenged on the grounds that they fail to mobilise and empower broader publics. The focus on relatively small numbers of partici-pants undermines strategies to promote broader public deliberation. While I am entirely sympathetic to this goal of widespread empowerment, to my mind the critique misses the point in two ways. Social and economic dynamics, including the power of organised and entrenched interests, make it difficult to imagine what broader public deliberation around the interests of future generations might look like. Most participatory initiatives simply do not achieve the level of diversity of DMPs. Further, the power of DMPs is their capacity to bring everyday people into decision-making on strategic and complex issues. It is not clear how that can be achieved across large-scale mass publics, either in terms of motivating people or in terms of coordinating their action. DMPs offer a more realistic division of political labour: they draw a diverse sample from the population in order to undertake particularly intense policy tasks. Most people do not want to participate in politics most of the time! Emerging research on how the public conceives of DMPs is promising. The public appears to have trust and confidence in the decision-making capacities of DMPs, particularly when comparisons are drawn with established political institutions. This confidence rests either on identification with the 'ordinary people' who are selected or on the recognition that members have gained a level of expertise through the process such that they are well placed to make decisions.[15]

A final set of criticisms has more bite. What is the point of DMPs, if they fail to have impact on political decision-making? It is easy to point to exemplary cases – the impact of the Irish Citizens Assembly on the constitutional status of abortion in Ireland is, typically, the favoured example. Overlooked is the fate of the proposals on climate change made by the same assembly. Some were adopted, others seen as too radical, and hence ignored. The problem is how DMPs are 'coupled' with decision-making institutions. The commonly held view of DMPs is that they are particularly effective forms of public consultation: they provide politicians with high-quality inputs to inform their decision-making. That allows space for public authorities to commission DMPs on their own terms and to cherry-pick those recommendations they find politically acceptable. The way in which DMPs are integrated into the political system is a legitimate concern. It reminds us of Ostrom's assertion that participatory designs are most effective when participants are empowered. Empowered not just to make recommendations, but to shape the agenda and to make collective political decisions.

Emerging practice points to what empowered DMPs might look like. A new model of sortition governance has been introduced by the parliament of the German-speaking community in East Belgium. A permanent, randomly selected citizens' council is afforded the power to decide which issues need to be dealt with by a citizens' assembly. Parliament, government, civil society organisations, and citizens can offer suggestions, but the agenda-setting power rests with the council. Membership of that council rotates every few months, so that members serve only for one year. Separate citizens' assemblies are then established to analyse each of the designated topics, and their recommendations are then considered by the relevant parliamentary committees. The council is empowered to set the agenda, although the outputs of the assemblies have only recommendatory power. In a short-lived experiment in Madrid, a randomly selected body – the Observatorio – was empowered to consider proposals from citizens collected on a citywide digital platform and to commission referendums where it saw fit.[16]

When it comes to empowered decision-making, DMP practice in Poland is groundbreaking. Municipal mayors commit to implementing any decision that emerges from a citizens' assembly where support from members of the assembly is above 80 per cent. Below that figure, the mayor has discretion on whether to act.[17] Assemblies have been run on a number of issues, including flooding and LGBTQ+ rights, and a climate assembly is planned for Warsaw in 2020. The mayor's implementation of decisions from the citizens' assembly in Gdansk on flooding is widely recognised as ensuring more robust city defences.

As DMPs are used more extensively and become established sites of countervailing power, concerns will shift to whether they can remain protected spaces. As Michael Neblo suggests, political import will generate 'powerful incentives for interest groups and partisan elites to try to manipulate deliberative forums'.[18] The history of legal juries indicates the extent to which laws similar to those against jury tampering may be necessary to avoid external manipulation.

Pragmatic or radical participatory governance?

We can thus begin to unpack what pragmatic and more radical integration of DMPs into long-term governance might look like.

In the previous chapter I argued that the legitimacy of independent OFGs can be enhanced through public participation strategies in terms of the way these strategies both improve judgements about the interests of future generations and bolster the political capital of such independent agencies. DMPs could be a central element of that strategy. Individual citizens' assemblies could be organised to bring public judgement to bear on controversial issues faced by an OFG, or to consider issues with long-term consequences where public opinion is poorly structured. A permanent citizen panel where membership is rotated regularly could provide ongoing input into decision-making and public scrutiny of the actions of the OFG. A similar idea was instituted by the National Institute for Health and Care Excellent (NICE) in the United Kingdom, although the influence of the Citizens' Council was limited.[19] The Council was not given the time, resources, or critical tasks to have a significant impact on the agency's work. As the developments in Belgium and Poland suggest, such integration could be more radical, if a permanent panel is to be given the right to commission its own citizens' assemblies where it feels them to be necessary and if the OFG is to be expected to implement proposals when these are supported by a supermajority within such bodies. The potential for a more extensive and deeper public engagement in organisational governance is yet to be fully exploited by independent oversight bodies. The same is true for other parts of the political system: the terms under which mini-publics and other participatory forms are embedded are critical to ensuring that their timing, framing, and outputs impact on decision-making.

An even more radical step is the proposal for a randomly selected legislative chamber. The contention is that, by removing electoral party political motivations, a sortition legislature would be more sensitive to the interests of future genera-tions. At its most extreme, the call is to replace all elected politicians with randomly selected citizens.[20] More common is the argument for a second chamber in unicameral systems, for the replacement of hereditary or appointed chambers (e.g. the House of Lords) where they exist as part of bicameral systems, or even for an additional citizens' branch of government.[21] A sortition legis-lature could be mandated specifically to safeguard the future or we might reasonably expect long-term thinking to emerge, given what we know about deliberative processes.

Sympathetic critics raise concerns about this simple 'replacement' thesis – that is, about the idea that elected politicians could be replaced by randomly selected citizens without a signif-icant restructuring of the legislature. Neither our knowledge of ancient Athens nor our experience with contemporary mini-publics can be directly translated to the context of a legislature. Advocates fail to recognise that sortition works effectively when it occurs in combination with rapid rotation and limited mandates. Instead membership of a sortition legislature is usually proposed for two to four years, with an expansive mandate to consider all areas of public policy. There are good reasons to expect that replacing elected politicians with randomly selected citizens will not have the desired effects. Longer terms of office and a broad mandate are likely to generate adverse effects such as horse-trading, undue influence from external interests, and bureaucratic capture that will undermine deliberative qualities. Sortition legislatures are likely to be dominated by elected chambers where the latter remain in place.[22]

If sortition is to play a role at a legislative level, then the form and structure of legislative institutions need to be reconsidered at the same time. How might legislative functions be undertaken effectively, but without losing the critical elements of sortition, rotation, and limited mandate? Lessons can be drawn from processes such as participatory budgeting. Its effectiveness in Brazil has rested on a separation between agenda setting, scrutiny, and rule-making.[23] The designers of the original participatory budget in Porto Alegre realised that rule-making needed to happen in a different type of participatory space from that of demand making that came from local communities. Rule-making occurred before any demands were put forward, and this ensured that game-playing would be kept at a minimum. In this way, Porto Alegre and other Brazilian municipalities were able to embed rules of distribution that embodied social justice rather than the short-term interests of particular communities. The separation between agenda setting and scrutiny is the basis of the new East Belgium model discussed earlier, where the citizens' council plays an agenda-setting role in selecting topics for consideration and separate citizens' assemblies undertake scrutiny of the issues selected.

Alternative legislative sortition proposals have emerged that recognise these different institutional functions. I have argued, with David Owen, that second chambers could be replaced with a more popular and participatory institution, made up of 6,000 citizens selected randomly on an annual basis.[24] When proposals for new or revised laws or policies come from the elected chamber or some other source (whether it be a direct democratic device or another randomly selected body, as in

East Belgium), an assembly of 100–200 is drawn randomly from the pool of 6,000. At the same time, lead facilitators are randomly assigned to the assembly. The practice of rapid rotation would not only extend participation, but also help to protect against external manipulation. Where the assembly supports the proposal with a super-majority, the proposal becomes law. If rejected by a supermajority, the proposal is abandoned. Where support is between these figures, the proposal is returned to the first chamber to reconsider. Terrill Bouricius has offered a more systematic plan to embed 'multi-body sortition'.[25] He separates out the different functions of a legislature and then designs bodies to play those functions. This leads to a series of different sortition institutions such as agenda council, review panels, policy jury, rules council and oversight council. Bouricius recognises that it is incredibly unlikely that his blueprint could be implemented in one fell swoop: sortition does not have enough recognition and legitimacy, and the alternative model is complex to articulate. His take is that the first stage in moving to a more sortiton-based system is to 'peel away issues' from the legislature and to move them to sortition bodies.

This 'peeling away' strategy is in the process of emerging in climate politics. Extinction Rebellion

(XR) is demanding a national citizens' assembly on the climate and ecological emergency that would be empowered to take decisions to ensure that the United Kingdom realises a rapid decarbonisation path and halts biodiversity loss.[26] This is explicitly influenced by the Polish practice of citizens' assemblies, where mayors commit to adopting those proposals that have significant support within the body. The French Citizens' Convention on Climate Change takes us some way towards XR's demand. In response to street protests against his proposal for a carbon tax, President Macron commissioned the convention to make recommendations as to how France can reduce its greenhouse gas emissions by at least 40 per cent by 2030 in a spirit of social justice.[27] The 150 selected citizens met over seven weekends, delivering their extensive recommendations in June 2020. Macron has promised 'no filter'; proposals for laws, regulations, and referendums are to be considered directly by parliament and the president. This still leaves the authorities with room to manoeuvre. Politicians find it hard to give up their power. At the same time, they seem incapable of making the tough decisions necessary to deal with long-term policy issues. If citizens' assemblies prove their worth in relation to climate change, empowered assemblies in other policy domains may follow.

The contours of pragmatic and radical strategies for deepening democracy begin to take shape. The pragmatic path follows well-established practice, DMPs playing a more consultative role and providing public judgements on long-term policy challenges for politicians and other public officials to consider. This may help to break democratic myopia. It can give politicians 'cover' to act more decisively on politically contentious issues. However, pragmatic participatory strategy generates an interesting paradox, which is likely to limit its effect. Issues are being handed over to DMPs because of the structured short-termism of the commissioning authority. When the DMP comes to making its recommendations, these are then passed back to the very institution and political actors who continue to be subject to the drivers of short-termism. Occasionally the DMP may be what it takes to shift political calculations and enable long-term action. But relying on existing institutions to operate more effectively cannot be a systematic response to democratic myopia.

A more radical deepening of democracy for future generations looks to empower the spaces for participation and deliberation. This means empowering them in their capacity both to shape the issues under consideration and to ensure the implementation of proposals that have widespread support within the body. We are dealing here with a more disruptive political strategy – one that brings into question the dominant position of established democratic institutions. The record of these institutions is so poor that a radical strategy may be a necessity.

DMPs can operate at any level of governance, provided that additional resources are made available for translation. A small number of experiments have taken place at the European level that provide evidence that language and nationality are not necessarily barriers to participatory engagement.[28] Proposals have emerged for the use of DMPs to scrutinise the activities of existing transnational organisations such as the World Bank and International Monetary Fund.[29] If a European or global-level OFG were to emerge, it could become, again, the champion of participation through the use of DMPs. The barrier is our imagination, creativity, and political will, not the boundaries of the nation state.

Conclusion

A participatory approach to deepening democracy for the long term cannot be based on DMPs alone.

We need to go through a similar exercise of considering the long-term potential of other participatory institutions and devices – digital and face-to-face ones, as well as ones that blend the two media. We need to be creative in thinking how different approaches can be coupled in participatory systems. We need room for experimenting. For example, the Future Design movement in Japan is using DMP-type processes, but splits the selected group into two. One group analyses the issue, as usual; the other is asked to think itself into the position of people who would be living in 50 years' time. The two groups work independently and then bring their ideas together, to develop a common strategy. Evidence suggests that outcomes are qualitatively different in the way the future is conceived of and envisaged.[30]

We need to think not only about the traditional political realm, but about how we can design participatory processes within other centres of power, including economic organisations. The ambition of this chapter is to show – using the example of DMPs – that resources exist for thinking creatively about future generations and, importantly, for realising a participatory politics on their behalf.

The currently dominant strategies for designing democratic institutions to protect future generations are wrong-headed. They miss a critical element: the direct involvement of the people. Designing institutions that bring citizens front and centre into the decision-making process is a strategy for long-term governance that sits at odds with the orthodoxy of focusing on ways of reforming the structure and practices of legislatures, adopting constitutional provisions, and creating new independent offices for future generations. These strategies need to be blended. The promise is a reinvigorated democracy that deals effectively with long-term policy challenges – a reinvigorated democracy we would be proud to pass on to future generations.

Afterword

Democratic Design for Future Generations

Can democracy safeguard the future? This book suggests that it can, but only if democratic institutions are designed to ameliorate the drivers of short-termism. The core defining feature of contemporary democracies – elections – generates governing bodies that are particularly myopic. Future generations have no voice within elected assemblies. Electoral cycles generate incentives for politicians to prioritise short-term returns, and make it difficult for the public to have confidence that long-term promises will be delivered. Entrenched interest groups are able to shape the agenda so as to protect their advantages. The broader capitalist system reinforces short-term thinking and action. It is as if elected bodies had been designed explicitly to undermine a long-term orientation in democratic politics.

The suggestions offered in this book are in no way exhaustive. The focus on independent offices for future generations (OFGs) and on deliberative mini-publics (DMPs) is illustrative. The decision to select these two institutional forms for a detailed consideration is due to the fact that examples already exist. Although currently these are fairly marginal political institutions within democracies, we can draw lessons from their practice. The analysis of the limits of legislatures and of the potential role of constitutions, OFGs, and DMPs generates a number of principles that can be drawn upon to guide institutional design. Again, these principles are not exhaustive. Rather they give us some direction as to how we might craft democratic spaces that promote consideration of the long term and of the interests of future generations.

Independence. The creation of institutions independent of electoral party and interest group motivations provides the space for contesting short-termism. Sortition, when combined with rotation, offers one way of selecting democratically decision makers who are independent and not subject to the pressures that face elected politicians.

116

Diversity. When the vulnerable and politically marginalised are not present within political institutions, their interests are rarely considered systematically, and this has a detrimental impact on their well-being. Their absence also means that their perspectives on the interests of future generations are not considered, which increases the likelihood that inequalities are reproduced across generations. Where voices from across all social groups are present in decision-making in all their diversity, different perspectives on long-term policy are brought to bear.

Deliberation. The tendency of people is to overlook the long term in their everyday practices, as broader social forces and unreflective instincts dominate. Deliberation encourages slow thinking and reflection on the interests of others, including future generations. Deliberation creates the political conditions to challenge the status quo and to enable collective political judgement for the long term.

Institutionalisation. Compliance with political decisions over time requires permanent bodies that promote long-term thinking. The danger is that temporary spaces are created in which far-sighted recommendations are made, but then the implementation of decisions is left to institutions that are subject to short-term pressures.

Empowerment. Too often institutions that bring forward long-term proposals have only an advisory or consultative role in the democratic system. Bodies that are created to defend and promote the interests of future generations need to have decision-making power – or at least the capacity to veto or delay decisions that fail to consider the impact of policy on those yet unborn.

If political spaces are created that embody these design principles, the capacity of democracies to consider the long term and to safeguard the interests of future generations will be enhanced. The promise is for a more robust democracy, both now and in the future.

Further Reading

How democratic institutions can be designed to ameliorate short-termism is a relatively underdeveloped field of study. Philosophers have long debated the characteristics of intergenerational justice and the obligations we owe to future generations. Economists, psychologists, and sociologists have offered competing accounts of our time preferences. The study of the institutional settings within which democracies can better consider the interests of future generations has lagged by comparison. Much of the work carried out in this area has emerged only in recent years, some significant contributions still being in the pipeline.

An excellent place to start is the collection *Institutions for Future Generations* edited by Iñigo González-Ricoy and Axel Gosseries (Oxford University Press, 2016). It brings together an impressive array of authors, mostly with a background in political philosophy, who offer theoretically sophisticated analyses of different institutional proposals. The introduction by the editors and a chapter on the drivers of short-termism by Michael MacKenzie set the scene for the institutional proposals that follow, a number of which are analysed in this book.

An exhaustive study of the field can be found in Jonathan Boston's impressive book *Governing for the Future: Designing Democratic Institutions for a Better Tomorrow* (Emerald, 2016). On the basis of extensive research and interviews, Boston conceptualises and assesses the source of what he terms the 'presentist bias', lays out principles designed to guide long-term democratic governance, and surveys and assesses options for institutional reform.

A forthcoming book by Michael MacKenzie, *Future Publics: Democracy, Deliberation and Future-Regarding Action* (Oxford University Press, 2021), represents the first systematic analysis of the causes and response to democratic myopia from within democratic theory. MacKenzie asks why this area of work has been dominated by justice theorists and makes the case that deliberative democracy in particular is well suited to responding to the demands of long-term governance. He ends the book with reflections on institutional design.

A fascinating book aimed at a more general readership but no less sophisticated in its analysis is *The Good Ancestor: How to Think Long Term in a Short-Term World* (Penguin, 2020), by the well-known public philosopher Roman Krznaric. The book engagingly offers the reader a history of short-termism, explaining candidly how we lost sight of the future. Krznaric reflects on the design of democratic, economic, and social institutions and suggests practical ways in which we, as individuals, can change our thinking.

An author who has made a number of important contributions to the field but whose book is still in gestation is Simon Caney. His essay for the Centre for Sustainable Prosperity, 'Democratic Reform, Intergenerational Justice and the Challenges for the Long Term' (2019), gives a taste of the extended analysis that will follow.

Different policy areas have seen a number of studies that touch on the question of how consideration of the long term could be more effectively embedded. Alan Jacobs's *Governing for the Long Term: Democracy and the Politics of Investment* (Cambridge University Press, 2011) is a compelling and highly nuanced comparative analysis of the development of pensions policies in a number of democratic states. Also, Jacobs and Scott Matthews have co-authored a couple of significant articles that challenge the economic orthodoxy of discounting in relation to political preferences – for example 'Why Do Citizens Discount the Future? Public Opinion and the Timing of Policy Consequences', *British Journal of Political Science* 42.4 (2012): 903–35.

A growing literature explores the relationship between democracy and the climate crisis. Frank Fischer's *Climate Crisis and the Democratic Prospect: Participatory Governance in Sustainable Communities* (Oxford University Press, 2017) offers both theoretical and practical reflections, making the case for a radical 'relocalisation'. Daniel J. Fiorino, *Can Democracy Handle Climate Change?* (Polity, 2018), in the same series as the present book, recognises the challenges facing democratic governance and provides a rigorous defence against authoritarian alternatives. In *Democracy and Climate Change* (London: Routledge: 2018), Frederic Hanusch offers a systematic analysis of how qualities of democracy influence performance in national climate policies.

The Too Difficult Box: The Big Issues Politicians Can't Crack (Biteback, 2014) is an engaging collection edited by Charles Clarke, the former UK government minister. He brings together chapters written by a range of politicians and former civil servants with personal experience in trying to confront long-term policy problems across diverse domains. The collection offers an insight, at times disturbing, into the adversarial short-termism that afflicts our political culture.

The *Intergenerational Justice Review* is, as the name suggests, a journal preoccupied with questions of justice and carries occasional articles on democracy and institutional design. The website of the charity the Foundation for Democracy and Sustainable Development (FDSD), currently chaired by this author, provides extensive material on a range of proposals for long-term democratic governance (see https://www.fdsd.org).

Notes

Notes to Chapter 1

1 Intergovernmental Panel on Climate Change, *Special report: Global warming of 1.5°C* (Geneva: IPPC, 2018). https://www.ipcc.ch/sr15.

2 Committee on Climate Change, *Net zero: The UK's contribution to stopping global warming* (London: Committee on Climate Change, May 2019). https://www.theccc.org.uk/publication/net-zero-the-uks-contribution-to-stopping-global-warming. The United Kingdom was the first country to commit legally to reduction of greenhouse gases. The Climate Change Act 2008 initially committed the government to reductions of 80 per cent of the 1990 emission levels by 2050. More recently, in 2019, the government adopted a 2050 net zero target.

3 Tim Elwell-Sutton, Adam Tinson, Claire Greszczuk, David Finch, Erica Holt-White, Grace Everest, Nadya Mihaylova, Suzanne Wood, and Jo Biddy, *Creating healthy lives: A whole government*

approach to long-term investment in the nation's health (London: Health Foundation, September 2019), p. 4.

4 Daniel R. Coats, *Statement for the record: Worldwide threat assessment of the US Intelligence Community* (Senate Select Committee on Intelligence, 2019). https://www.dni.gov/files/ODNI/documents/2019-ATA-SFR---SSCI.pdf.

5 Global Preparedness Monitoring Board, *A world at risk: Annual report on global preparedness for health emergencies* (Geneva: Global Preparedness Monitoring Board, 2019).

6 Charles Clarke (ed.), *The too difficult box: The big issues politicians can't crack* (London: Biteback Publishing, 2014); Martin Rees, *On the future: Prospects for humanity* (Princeton, NJ: Princeton University Press, 2018).

7 Sarah Breeden, 'Avoiding the storm: Climate change and the financial system'. Speech delivered to the Official Monetary & Financial Institutions Forum, April 2019. https://www.bankofengland.co.uk/-/media/boe/files/speech/2019/avoiding-the-storm-climate-change-and-the-financial-system-speech-by-sarah-breeden.pdf.

8 Nicholas Stern, *The economics of climate change: The Stern review* (Cambridge: Cambridge University Press, 2014).

9 Andrew Healy and Neil Malhotra, 'Myopic voters and natural disaster policy', *American Political Science Review* 103.3 (2009): 387–406.

10 Simon Caney, 'Climate change and the future:

Discounting for time, wealth and risk', *Journal of Social Policy* 40.2 (2009): 163–86, here p. 171.

11 For alternative formulations of the determinants of democratic myopia, see Michael K. MacKenzie, 'Institutional design and sources of short-termism', in Iñigo González-Ricoy and Axel Gosseries (eds), *Institutions for future generations* (Oxford: Oxford University Press, 2016), pp. 24–48; Simon Caney, 'Democratic reform, intergenerational justice and the challenges of the long term' (CUSP Essay Series on the Morality of Sustainable Prosperity, No 11, 2019). https://www.cusp.ac.uk /themes/m/m1-11.

12 Anne Phillips, *The politics of presence* (Oxford: Oxford University Press, 2003), p. 13.

13 Anja Karnein, 'Can we represent future generations?', in Iñigo González-Ricoy and Axel Gosseries (eds), *Institutions for future generations* (Oxford: Oxford University Press, 2016), pp. 83–97.

14 William D. Nordhaus, 'The political business cycle', *Review of Economic Studies* 42.2 (1975): 169–90; James E. Alt and David Dreyer Lassen, 'Transparency, political polarization, and political budget cycles in OECD countries', *American Journal of Political Science* 50.3 (2006): 530–50.

15 Healy and Malhotra, 'Myopic voters and natural disaster policy'.

16 Alan M. Jacobs and J. Scott Matthews, 'Why do citizens discount the future? Public opinion and the timing of policy consequences', *British Journal of Political Science* 42.4 (2012): 903–35.

17 Sabine Pahl, Stephen Sheppard, Christine Boomsma,

and Christopher Groves, 'Perceptions of time in relation to climate change', *Wiley Interdisciplinary Reviews: Climate Change* 5.3 (2014): 375–88; Shane Frederick, George Loewenstein, and Ted O'Donoghue, 'Time discounting and time preference: A critical review', *Journal of Economic Literature* 40.2 (2002): 351–401; Daniel Kahneman, *Thinking, fast and slow* (London: Macmillan, 2011).

18 Dennis F. Thompson, 'Representing future generations: Political presentism and democratic trusteeship', *Critical Review of International Social and Political Philosophy* 13.1 (2010): 17–37, here p. 17.

19 Frederick et al., 'Time discounting and time preference'; Hilary J. Graham, Martin Bland, Richard Cookson, Mona Kanaan, and Piran C. L. White, 'Do people favour policies that protect future generations? Evidence from a British Survey of Adults', *Journal of Social Policy* 46.3 (2017): 423–45.

20 Kahneman, *Thinking, fast and slow*.

21 Healy and Malhotra, 'Myopic voters and natural disaster policy'.

22 Jacobs and Matthews, 'Why do citizens discount the future?'.

23 Will Jennings, Gerry Stoker, and Joe Twyman, 'The dimensions and impact of political discontent in Britain', *Parliamentary Affairs* 69.4 (2016): 876–900.

24 Thomas Tozer, *A new intergenerational contract: Intergenerational justice in principle and policy* (London: Intergenerational Foundation, 2019).

https://www.if.org.uk/wp-content/uploads/2019/03/
A-New-Intergenerational-Contract_defin.pdf.

25 Quoted in Naomi Klein, *This changes everything: Capitalism vs the climate* (London: Penguin, 2015), p. 151.

26 Martin Gilens and Benjamin I. Page, 'Testing theories of American politics: Elites, interest groups, and average citizens', *Perspectives on Politics* 12.3 (2014): 564–81.

27 Haroon Chowdry and Carey Oppenheim, *Spending on late intervention: How we can do better for less* (London: Early Intervention Foundation, 2015). https://www.eif.org.uk/report/spending-on-late-intervention-how-we-can-do-better-for-less.

28 David Runciman, *The confidence trap: A history of democracy in crisis from World War I to the present*, rev. edn (Princeton, NJ: Princeton University Press, 2017).

29 Kym Irving, 'Overcoming short-termism: Mental time travel, delayed gratification and how not to discount the future', *Australian Accounting Review* 19.4 (2009): 278–94; Dominic Barton, Jonathan Bailey, and Joshua Zoffer, *Rising to the challenge of short-termism* (Boston, MA: FCLT Global, 2016). https://www.fcltglobal.org/docs/default-source/default-document-library/fclt-global-rising-to-the-challenge.pdf?sfvrsn=0.

30 William Ophuls, *Ecology and the politics of scarcity* (San Francisco, CA: W. H. Freeman, 1977), p. 224; see also Robert Heilbroner, *An inquiry into the human prospect* (London: Calder & Boyars, 1974).

31 David J.C. Shearman and Joseph Wayne Smith, *The climate change challenge and the failure of democracy* (Westport, CT: Greenwood Publishing Group, 2007).

32 James Lovelock, 'Humans are too stupid to prevent climate change', *Guardian*, 29 March 2010. https://www.theguardian.com/science/2010/mar/29/james-lovelock-climate-change.

33 Martin Rees, 'If I ruled the world', *Prospect*, 21 August 2014. http://www.prospectmagazine.co.uk/regulars/if-i-ruled-the-world-martin-rees.

34 Jamie McQuilkin, 'Doing justice to the future: A global index of intergenerational solidarity derived from national statistics', *Intergenerational Justice Review* 4.1 (2016): 42–1; Roman Krznaric, *The good ancestor: How to think long term in a short-term world* (London: Penguin, 2020).

35 Frederic Hanusch, *Democracy and climate change* (London: Routledge, 2018).

36 In his study of pensions reform, Jacobs argues that the existence of veto points explains why some democracies have developed more effective long-term policy. See Alan M. Jacobs, *Governing for the long term: Democracy and the politics of investment* (Cambridge: Cambridge University Press, 2011).

37 Daniel J. Fiorino, *Can democracy handle climate change?* (Cambridge: Polity, 2018).

38 Roberto Stefan Foa and Yascha Mounk, 'The danger of deconsolidation', *Journal of Democracy* 27.3 (2016): 5–17.

39 John Dewey, *The public and its problems: An essay*

in political inquiry (New York: Henry Holt, 1927), p. 327.

Notes to Chapter 2

1 A limitation of the analysis that follows is its focus on institutional practices in established democracies and its reliance on western democratic thought. An extended analysis would draw on creative democratic thinking and practices from other traditions.

2 Alan M. Jacobs, *Governing for the long term: Democracy and the politics of investment* (Cambridge: Cambridge University Press, 2011).

3 Lori M. Poloni-Staudinger, 'Are consensus democracies more environmentally effective?', *Environmental Politics* 17.3 (2008): 410–30; Peter Christoff and Robyn Eckersley, 'Comparing state responses', in Peter Christoff, Robyn Eckersley, John S. Dryzek, et al. (eds), *The Oxford handbook of climate change and society* (Oxford: Oxford University Press, 2011), pp. 431–48.

4 Vesa Koskimaa and Tapio Raunio, 'Encouraging a longer time horizon: The Committee for the Future in the Finnish eduskunta', *Journal of Legislative Studies* 26.2 (2020): 159–79; Brian Groombridge, 'Parliament and the future: Learning from Finland', *Political Quarterly* 77.2 (2006): 273–80.

5 Foundation for Democracy and Sustainable Development, 'A proposal: House of Lords Committee for Future Generations', March 2018.

https://www.fdsd.org/wp-content/uploads/2018/04/
HoLCommittee-Proposal.pdf.

6 Visit https://publications.parliament.uk/pa/bills/lbill/
2019-2019/0015/20015.pdf.

7 Visit http://scotlandfutureforum.org; see also
Groombridge, 'Parliament and the future'.

8 Martin Gilens and Benjamin I. Page, 'Testing theories
of American politics: Elites, interest groups, and
average citizens', *Perspectives on Politics* 12.3
(2014): 564–81.

9 Philippe van Parijs, 'The disfranchisement of the
elderly, and other attempts to secure intergenerational justice', *Philosophy & Public Affairs* 27.4
(1998): 292–333.

10 David Runciman, 'Democracy for young people',
Talking Politics, 5 December 2018. https://www.
talkingpoliticspodcast.com/blog/2018/129-
democracy-for-young-people.

11 Juliana Bidadanure, 'Can young people act as proxies
for future generations?', in Iñigo González-Ricoy and
Axel Gosseries (eds), *Institutions for future generations* (Oxford: Oxford University Press, 2016), pp.
266–81; van Parijs, 'The disfranchisement of the
elderly'.

12 Andrew Dobson, 'Representative democracy and
the environment', in William M. Lafferty and James
Meadowcroft (eds), *Democracy and the Environment*
(Cheltenham: Edward Elgar, 1996), pp. 124–39.

13 Kristian Skagen Ekeli, 'Green constitutionalism:
The constitutional protection of future generations',
Ratio Juris 20.3 (2007): 378–401.

14 Kristian Ekeli, 'Constitutional experiments: Representing future generations through subma-jority rules', *Journal of Political Philosophy* 17.4 (2009): 440–61; 'Electoral design, sub-majority rules, and representation for future generations', in Iñigo González-Ricoy and Axel Gosseries (eds), *Institutions for future generations* (Oxford: Oxford University Press, 2016), pp. 214–27.

15 Ekeli, 'Constitutional experiments', p. 445.

16 Michael K. MacKenzie, 'A general-purpose, randomly selected chamber', in Iñigo González-Ricoy and Axel Gosseries (eds), *Institutions for future genera-tions* (Oxford: Oxford University Press, 2016), pp. 282–98.

17 John Gastil and Erik Olin Wright, *Legislature by lot: Transformative designs for deliberative governance* (London: Verso, 2019).

18 Robyn Eckersley, 'Deliberative democracy, ecological representation and risk: Towards a democracy of the affected', in Michael Saward (ed.), *Democratic innovation* (London: Routledge, 2003), pp. 131–46.

19 United Nations General Assembly, *Report of the United Nations Conference on Environment and Development* (New York: United Nations, 1992). https://www.un.org/en/development/desa/population/migration/generalassembly/docs/globalcompact/A_CONF.151_26_Vol.I_Declaration.pdf.

20 Iñigo González-Ricoy, 'Constitutionalizing inter-generational provisions', in Iñigo González-Ricoy and Axel Gosseries (eds), *Institutions for future*

generations (Oxford: Oxford University Press, 2016), pp. 170–84.

21 Iñigo González-Ricoy and Felipe Rey, 'Enfranchising the future: Climate justice and the representation of future generations', *Wiley Interdisciplinary Reviews: Climate Change* 10.5 (2019): 1–12.

22 Bernd Süssmuth and Robert K. von Weizsäcker, 'Institutional determinants of public debt: A political economy perspective', in Joerg C. Tremmel (ed.), *Handbook of intergenerational justice* (Cheltenham: Edward Elgar, 2006), pp. 170–84; Joerg C. Tremmel, 'Establishing intergenerational justice in national constitutions', in Joerg Chet Tremmel (ed.), *Handbook of intergenerational justice* (Cheltenham: Edward Elgar, 2006), pp. 187–214.

23 Ekeli, 'Green constitutionalism', p. 388.

24 Jeremy Waldron, 'The core of the case against judicial review', *Yale Law Journal* 115 (2005): 1346–406.

25 Ekeli, 'Green constitutionalism'.

Notes to Chapter 3

1 This and the next chapter draw on the arguments in Graham Smith, 'Enhancing the legitimacy of offices for future generations: The case for public participation', *Political Studies* 2020. doi: 10.1177/0032321719885100.

2 Visit https://www.theccc.org.uk.

3 Committee on Climate Change, *Net Zero: The UK's contribution to stopping global warming* (London: Committee on Climate Change, 2019). https://

www.theccc.org.uk/publication/net-zero-the-uks-contribution-to-stopping-global-warming.

4 Visit https://www.nic.org.uk.

5 Shlomo Shoham, *Future intelligence* (Gütersloh: Bertelsman Stifung, 2010), p. 124.

6 Na'ama Teschner, *Official bodies that deal with the needs of future generations and sustainable development* (Jerusalem: Knesset Information and Research Center, 2013), p. 3. https://m.knesset.gov.il/EN/activity/mmm/me03194.pdf.

7 Shoham, *Future intelligence*, p. 105.

8 Drawn from an unpublished interview undertaken by the author with Sándor Fülöp, former Hungarian Parliamentary Commissioner for Future Generations, in 2017.

9 Visit http://www.ajbh.hu/en/web/ajbh-en.

10 Visit https://futuregenerations.wales.

11 Visit https://futuregenerations.wales/news/future-generations-commissioner-for-wales-welcomes-brave-decision-by-first-minister-on-the-m4-relief-road.

12 Martin Nesbit and Andrea Illés, *Establishing an EU 'Guardian for Future Generations': Report and recommendations for the World Future Council* (London: Institute for European Environmental Policy, 2015); Halina Ward, *Committing to the future we want: A High Commissioner for Future Generations at Rio+20: Discussion Paper* (London: Foundation for Democracy and Future Generations and World Futures Council, 2012). https://www.fdsd.org/wp-content/uploads/2014/11/Committing-to-the-future-we-want-main-report.pdf.

13 Pierre Rosanvallon, *Counter-democracy: Politics in an age of distrust* (Cambridge: Cambridge University Press, 2008), p. 85.

14 Kristian Skagen Ekeli, 'Green constitutionalism: The constitutional protection of future generations', *Ratio Juris* 20.3 (2007): 378–401.

15 Jason Brennan, *Against democracy* (Princeton, NJ: Princeton University Press, 2016).

16 Jonathan Boston, *Governing for the future: Designing democratic institutions for a better tomorrow* (Bingley: Emerald, 2016), p. 330.

17 Ibid., p. 331.

18 Ekeli, 'Green constitutionalism'.

19 Ludvig Beckman and Fredrik Uggla, 'An ombudsman for future generations', in Iñigo González-Ricoy and Axel Gosseries (eds), *Institutions for future generations* (Oxford: Oxford University Press, 2016), pp. 117–34, here p. 123.

20 Visit https://www.unece.org/env/pp/treatytext.html.

21 Hungarian Parliamentary Commissioner for Future Generations, *Comprehensive summary of the report of the Hungarian Parliamentary Commissioner for Future Generations, 2010* (Budapest: HPCFG, 2011); Hungarian Parliamentary Commissioner for Future Generations, *Comprehensive summary of the report of the Hungarian Parliamentary Commissioner for Future Generations, 2011* (Budapest: HPCFG, 2012).

22 Visit https://www.futurepolicy.org/equity-and-dignity/guardians/wales-well-being-of-future-generations-act.

23 Future Generations Commissioner for Wales, *Strategic Plan 2017–2023* (Cardiff: FGCW, 2017), p. 6.

https://futuregenerations.wales/wp-content/uploads/2018/11/2018-01-03-Strategic-Plan-FINAL.pdf.

24 Ibid., p. 6.

25 Ibid., p. 8.

26 Colin Scott, 'Accountability in the regulatory state', *Journal of Law & Society* 27.1 (2000): 38–60.

27 Shoham, *Future intelligence*, p. 105.

28 Shlomo Shoham and Nira Lamay, 'Commission for Future Generations in the Knesset: Lessons learnt', in Joerg C. Tremmel (ed.), *Handbook of intergenerational justice* (Cheltenham: Edward Elgar, 2006), pp. 244–81, here p. 225.

29 Pierre Rosanvallon, *Democratic legitimacy: Impartiality, reflexivity, proximity* (Princeton, NJ: Princeton University Press, 2011), p. 88.

30 Anja Karnein, 'Can we represent future generations?', in Iñigo González-Ricoy and Axel Gosseries (eds), *Institutions for future generations* (Oxford: Oxford University Press, 2016), pp. 83–97.

31 Quotation from an unpublished interview undertaken by the author with Sándor Fülöp, former Hungarian Parliamentary Commissioner for Future Generations, in 2017.

Notes to Chapter 4

1 Janna Thompson, *Intergenerational justice: Rights and responsibilities in an intergenerational polity* (London: Routledge, 2009).

2 Dennis F. Thompson, 'Representing future generations: Political presentism and democratic trusteeship',

Critical Review of International Social and Political Philosophy 13.1 (2010): 17–37, here p. 26.

3 Ibid., pp. 26–7.

4 Graham Smith, *Democratic innovations: Designing institutions for citizen participation* (Cambridge: Cambridge University Press, 2009), pp. 30–71.

5 Elinor Ostrom, *Governing the commons: The evolution of institutions for collective action* (Cambridge: Cambridge University Press, 1990).

6 Claus Offe and Ulrich K. Preuss, 'Democratic institutions and moral resources', in David Held (ed.), *Political Theory Today* (Cambridge: Polity, 1991), pp. 143–71.

7 Michael K. McKenzie, 'Deliberation and long-term decisions: Representing future generations', in André Bächtiger, John S. Dryzek, Jane Mansbridge, and Mark E. Warren (eds), *The Oxford handbook of deliberative democracy* (Oxford: Oxford University Press, 2018), pp. 251–69.

8 Kimmo Grönlund, André Bächtiger, and Maija Setälä (eds), *Deliberative mini-publics: Involving citizens in the democratic process* (Colchester: ECPR Press, 2014); Maija Setälä and Graham Smith, 'Mini-publics and deliberative democracy', in André Bächtiger, John S. Dryzek, Jane Mansbridge, and Mark E. Warren (eds), *The Oxford handbook of deliberative democracy* (Oxford: Oxford University Press, 2018), pp. 300–14; Smith, *Democratic innovations*. For the variety of designs and applications of deliberative mini-publics, see the work of members of Democracy R&D, at https://democracyrd.org.

9 The Democracy R&D platform provides links to the work of the Danish Board of Technology Foundation (Denmark), Involve (United Kingdom), MASS LPB (Canada), and New Democracy (Australia) among other bodies that have organised DMPs on aspects of long-term policy. See https://democracyrd.org.

10 James S. Fishkin, *Democracy when the public are thinking: Revitalizing our politics through public deliberation* (Oxford: Oxford University Press, 2018).

11 Kersty Hobson and Simon Niemeyer, 'Public responses to climate change: The role of deliberation in building capacity for adaptive action', *Global Environmental Change* 21.3 (2011): 957–71; Mikko Rask, Richard Worthington, and Lammi Minna (eds), *Citizen participation in global environmental governance* (London: Routledge, 2013); Lorelei L. Hanson (ed.), *Public deliberation on climate change: Lessons from Alberta Climate Change Dialogues* (Edmonton: Athabasca University Press, 2018). https://jefferson-center.org/rural-climate-dialogues.

12 Graham Smith, 'Citizens' assemblies: How to bring the wisdom of the public to bear on the climate emergency', *The Conversation*, 26 June 2019. https://theconversation.com/citizens-assemblies-how-to-bring-the-wisdom-of-the-public-to-bear-on-the-climate-emergency-119117.

13 Hobson and Neimeyer, 'Public responses to climate change'; Michael K. Mackenzie and Mark E. Warren, 'Two trust-based uses of minipublics in democratic systems', in Jane Mansbridge and John

Parkinson (eds), *Deliberative systems* (Cambridge: Cambridge University Press, 2012), pp. 95–124; Simon Niemeyer and Julia Jennstål, 'The deliberative democratic inclusion of future generations', in Iñigo González-Ricoy and Axel Gosseries (eds), *Institutions for future generations* (Oxford: Oxford University Press, 2016), pp. 247–65; Karen Parkhill, Christina Demski, Catherine Butler, Alexa Spence, and Nick Pidgeon, *Transforming the UK energy system: Public values, attitudes and acceptability: Synthesis report* (London: UKERC, 2013).

14 David Owen and Graham Smith, 'Sortition, rotation, and mandate: Conditions for political equality and deliberative reasoning', *Politics & Society* 46.3 (2018): 419–34; republished in John Gastil and Erik Olin Wright (eds), *Legislature by lot: Transformative designs for deliberative governance* (London: Verso, 2019), pp. 279–99; Oliver Dowlen, *The political potential of sortition* (Exeter: Imprint Academic, 2008).

15 Mark E. Warren and John Gastil, 'Can deliberative minipublics address the cognitive challenges of democratic citizenship?', *Journal of Politics* 77.2 (2015): 562–74.

16 Graham Smith, 'Institutionalizing deliberative mini-publics in Madrid City and German speaking Belgium: The first steps', *ConstitutionNet*, 28 March 2019. http://constitutionnet.org/news/institutionalizing-deliberative-mini-publics-madrid-city-and-german-speaking-belgium-first.

17 Marcin Gerwin, *Citizens' assemblies: Guide to democracy that works* (Krakow: Open Plan

Foundation, 2018). https://citizensassemblies.org; Smith, 'Citizens' assemblies'.

18 Michael A. Neblo, *Deliberative democracy between theory and practice* (Cambridge: Cambridge University Press, 2015), p. 181.

19 Celia Davies, Margaret Wetherell, and Elizabeth Barnett, *Citizens at the centre: Deliberative participation in healthcare decisions* (Bristol: Policy Press, 2006); see also http://www.nice.org.uk/Get-Involved/Citizens-Council.

20 David van Reybrouck, *Against elections: The case for democracy* (London: Bodley Head, 2013); Brett Henning, *The end of politicians* (London: Unbound, 2017).

21 Michael K. MacKenzie, 'A general-purpose, randomly selected chamber', in Iñigo González-Ricoy and Axel Gosseries (eds), *Institutions for future generations* (Oxford: Oxford University Press, 2016), pp. 282–98. For more general debates on sortition legislatures, see the various contributions in John Gastil and Erik Olin Wright, *Legislature by lot: Transformative designs for deliberative governance* (London: Verso, 2019); Patrizia Nanz and Claus Leggewie, *No representation without consultation: A citizens' guide to participatory democracy* (Toronto: Between the Lines, 2019).

22 Owen and Smith, 'Sortition, rotation, and mandate'. Terrill G. Bouricius, 'Why hybrid bicameralism is not good for sortition', in John Gastil and Erik Olin Wright, *Legislature by lot: Transformative designs*

for deliberative governance (London: Verso, 2019), pp. 313–33.

23 Smith, *Democratic innovations*, pp. 30–71.

24 Owen and Smith, 'Sortition, rotation, and mandate'.

25 Terrill G. Bouricius, 'Democracy through multi-body sortition: Athenian lessons for the modern day', *Journal of Public Deliberation* 9.1 (2013). https://www.publicdeliberation.net/jpd/vol9/iss1/art11.

26 Visit https://rebellion.earth.

27 Visit https://www.conventioncitoyennepourleclimat.fr.

28 Graham Smith, 'The European Citizens' Assembly', in Alberato Alemanno and James Organ (eds), *Democratic participation in a citizens' Europe* (London: ECPR Press / Roman and Littlefield International, forthcoming).

29 John S. Dryzek, André Bächtiger, and Karolina Milewicz, 'Toward a deliberative global citizens' assembly', *Global Policy* 2.1 (2001): 33–42; Bruno S. Frey and Alois Stutzer, 'Strengthening the citizens' role in international organizations', *Review of International Organizations* 1.1 (2006): 27–43.

30 Keishiro Hara, Ritsuji Yoshioka, Masashi Kuroda, Shuji Kurimoto, and Tatsuyoshi Saijo, 'Reconciling intergenerational conflicts with imaginary future generations: Evidence from a participatory deliberation practice in a municipality in Japan', *Sustainability Science* 14 (2019): 1605–19. See also http://www.bbc.com/future/story/20190318-can-we-reinvent-democracy-for-the-long-term.